Stories in EDU: SAIL With A Fleet

Jason Bretzmann and Kenny Bosch
with
John Briese, Kailee Drewno, Julie Fishburn,
Josh Gauthier, Leigh Anne Geib,
Dennis Griffin, Jr., Teresa Gross,
Barbara Gruener, Kris Jenkins, Tracy Kelly,
Aubrey Jones, Sherrill Knezel,
Dr. Patricia Kolodnicki, Brian Kulak,
Dr. Robin Mclean, Chuck Moss, Brianne Neil,
Rachelle Dene Poth, Jon Spike

Copyright © 2018 The Bretzmann Group

All rights reserved
Stories in EDU: SAIL With A Fleet: First Voyage

ISBN: 0692143440
ISBN-13: 978-0692143445

DEDICATION

To those educators who create great stories with their students every day. To those who currently share their stories and to those who never had the chance to share beyond the walls of their buildings. We honor what you've done for your students and what you've created for our profession. In the pages that follow, we share a small piece of the tremendous daily work that real teachers do. Enjoy. You deserve it.

CONTENTS

Introduction — 1

Overcoming Obstacles

1. The Wi-Fi Didn't Work, So We Bought a Goat — 5
    Jason Bretzmann

2. Sketchnotes in the Middle of Awful — 9
    Sherrill Knezel

3. Purpose Combats Complacency — 13
    Julie Fishburn

4. Intentional Decisions to Avoid Being the Obstacle — 19
    Rachelle Dene Poth

5. We Are on This Journey Together — 25
    Dennis Griffin, Jr.

Relationships

6. FFA and High Expectations — 29
    Dr. Robin Mclean

7. Tiny Ripples of Hope Build a Current — 35
    Kris Jenkins

8. Discussing the Greatness Inside — 39
    Chuck Moss

9. We Need You. It's an Emergency. — 43
    Brian Kulak

10. Secret Handshakes and High Fives — 49
    Kailoe Drewno

11. The Midnight Hour is Close at Hand — 55
    Jon Spike

Hooks

12	A Salon with a View *Jason Bretzmann*	61
13	You Had Me at Hello *Kenny Bosch*	67
14	Puppet Master *Barbara Gruener*	71
15	Pitzen's Rules *Jason Bretzmann*	75
16	With a Little Help from Our Friends *Teresa Gross*	79

Educational Technology Use

17	She Was the Moose of Her People *Jason Bretzmann*	83
18	Show Me the Munny *Kenny Bosch*	87
19	Hello Kitty *Josh Gauthier*	93
20	Useful *In* School? Or Useful *Beyond* School? *Jason Bretzmann*	97
21	Oh the Places You Will Virtually Go *Kenny Bosch*	99
22	Triple Moving Kahoot! *Jason Bretzmann*	103

That One Kid...

23	On Our Honeymoon, Elliott Joins Us for Dinner *Jason Bretzmann*	107
24	Michael Becomes My Little Brother *Brianne Neil*	111
25	Tom Learns Sign Language *Tracy Kelly*	117
26	Jamie Bites Teachers *Dr. Patricia Kolodnicki*	121
27	Steve Builds His Confidence *John Briese*	125
28	Clarence Learns *And* Teaches *Leigh Anne Szczurek Geib*	129
29	Sidney and His Phone *Aubrey Jones*	132

ACKNOWLEDGMENTS

We would like to acknowledge Freepik.com for giving us the ability to include fun visuals at the beginning of each chapter. We also share a sincere appreciation for Robert Kennedy's "Ripple of Hope" speech, as it is the inspiration for the title of Chapter 7 of this book. In addition, we are grateful to Dr. Mark French for the opportunity to share an ongoing story that started because of his great idea. Finally, we thank the spouses, families, and friends of every educator as they support and encourage the work we do.

INTRODUCTION

It has been a journey. A journey of learning.

When I started to flip my class years ago, I eventually got connected with the #flipclass community on Twitter. Each week at the chat, I lurked and I learned. At some point I asked a question. Then I took the bold step to contribute as well. I answered a question and told what I was trying...and they liked it. I answered more. I asked more of my own questions. I shared.

I was knee-deep in it all: telling the stories of our experiences, our successes, and our "learning opportunities," all while sitting and discussing in the comfortable community-living-room of a Twitter chat. Yet, while it was happening, I realized that not all educators were using Twitter. But all educators could benefit from these stories, these practices, these technology tools. These people.

All educators have access to books. We *love* books! So via a book, I tried to share with the broader flipped learning community by collecting the stories of how teachers were doing the teaching and learning in their classrooms. I wanted to share, celebrate, and amplify the great stuff I was seeing on Twitter with more educators so they could also benefit from the awesomeness. In 2013, we published *Flipping 2.0: Practical Strategies for Flipping Your Class* with two chapters in each core academic area, plus chapters on mastery learning, elementary and middle school flipping, Google tools to help teachers use technology to support the learning, and more. Still, I didn't yet realize where the true power rests.

Since then we've published three other books including the book *Personalized PD: Flip Your Professional Development*. We started our own Personalized PD community on Twitter and beyond that pushed the movement toward a more learner-centered approach to professional learning for educators. What a movement it is! Still, I didn't yet realize where the true power rests.

As part of the Personalized PD movement, we started Patio PD and Fireside PD where educators come to my house to learn, to share, and to hear what and how others in the profession do their daily work. We tell stories, share ideas, build lessons together, and share tips from the miniscule to the mighty. Other educators have added their patios to our learning communities as well. Still, I didn't yet realize where the true power rests.

Now, this isn't just one big advertisement. I'm headed somewhere with this. Stay on board...

We loved the stories and people asked us how to get others started telling their stories so we created a game called *Personalized PD: Game of Stories*. It has question prompts on 52 standard playing cards and asks participants to tell their stories to the educators sitting around the table. After each set of stories, the person with the best story wins the card and gets to ask a new question. Powerful stories and great ideas, but we've never finished a game. It turns into too much good conversation and discussion. We get distracted by good stories. Still, I didn't yet realize where the true power rests.

Then to share more of those great stories with even more people, we created a podcast called *Stories in EDU*. Usually we have two hosts and one guest, and they tell stories from inside their classrooms or buildings. These are more great stories! They tell stories while others listen and reflect. Still, I didn't yet realize where the true power rests.

Then in an impromptu conversation in the hallway with fellow teacher Kenny Bosch, a revelation occurred. We were discussing Twitter, Patio PD, Fireside PD, *Game of Stories*, and *Stories in EDU*. I was talking about how we all learn so much from each other, and how great it is to learn about all of these things and see the progress of so many educators. At some point Kenny observed that it's not just about the growth and the learning or the sharing. He said that it's about the stories. It is about *the stories*. It's about what we realize, understand, and learn from the stories.

With that nudge, I finally realized where the power rests. All along it has been about the stories.

The power doesn't rest in the best practices, the technology tools, the engagement strategies, the videos, the projects, the lessons, or the myriad of other things going on here. The power rests in the stories.

It is in the story of the educator going through the process of the profession. The story of the educator making daily, hourly decisions. Sometimes, these are decisions in the moment that can impact the outcome of a life, a career, or an academic success-potential for a student. The power is in hearing the story and considering what we would do. In what we *did* do in that similar situation. The power is in how the story lets us reflect on our own values and practices, and lets us plan for what we'll do next.

The power comes from the story as it lets us celebrate other educators who made the right decisions and, in so doing, instructed each of us what to do as we move forward. It's about us hearing the story as we sit on the edge of our seat hoping it goes in the right direction and then pumping our fist in the air when it does. When we celebrate others' successes we cheer for them and we cheer for ourselves going forward. We get better equipped to make our decisions because we are connected to those who made similar choices. Seeing and solidifying our connectedness empowers each of us to take risks and boldly set out to sea in potentially choppy waters.

The power rests in the story. When we share our stories, we share the blood, sweat, and tears of the learning and teaching we've done. And believe me, we didn't get to our stories on day one, or by accident. There are a dozen other stories we could each tell where it was a learning experience instead of a success story. We don't share those others as much as we should, but sharing our best selves, our more completed selves, is probably more of what we need right now anyway.

In *Stories in EDU: SAIL With a Fleet,* we share, celebrate, and amplify the meaningful work that connects us to the other educators who do it on a daily basis in the classrooms throughout our communities. The power rests in their stories. And probably in yours, too.

In each story, we ask the author to Share An Important Lesson (SAIL) through the telling of their story. As we learn and connect with each other through these stories, it becomes increasingly clear that we are in this profession together. We need each other. We are better together. While it is true that it seems that we are alone with our students in our classrooms and buildings, it is also unflinchingly true that we SAIL together. We are a fleet of righteous ships sailing to conquer new lands of learning. To spread the awesomeness of the best of our profession. To enlighten, to energize, and to entertain. To share, celebrate, and amplify the meaningful stories of the others in the fleet. Their stories will grab you, inspire you, and show you the reach of the work we do.

Now I realize where the true power rests. And now it can stop resting.

Let's SAIL.

Jason Bretzmann
New Berlin, Wisconsin
August 2018

CHAPTER 1: OVERCOMING OBSTACLES

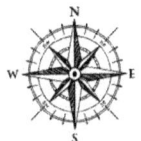

The Wi-Fi Didn't Work, So We Bought a Goat

by Jason Bretzmann

The Tuesday before winter break I had three activities planned for our high school civics class, and they all involved using the Wi-Fi. Unfortunately, the Wi-Fi didn't know that, and it decided to take the day off. Or as I told my students, "The 'Wi' was working fine; it was the 'Fi' that was a problem."

As I tried to figure out the problem and whether or not I could fix it, my students complained. Simultaneously I planned what we would do if I couldn't get a working internet connection. I grumbled under my breath as I tried different solutions and work-arounds. I may have been frustrated and disappointed that we couldn't do any of the things I had planned.

Half-heartedly, and probably less than half honestly, I suggested that when I get angry about the first world problems I have, I think about those who aren't concerned that they won't have Wi-Fi today. I told my students that when stuff like this happens I think about those who are more concerned about whether or not their family will have dinner tonight. Or about whether members of their family or their entire village will continue to survive. Flippantly I said that maybe we should stop complaining and buy those other people a goat. My students said, "What?"

To explain what I meant, I introduced my students to Heifer International®, a charitable organization based on the premise that if you give livestock to families in extremely poor countries, they will benefit from the added nutrition and income from the milk and cheese produced. I continued that it would add to the viability of the whole village if there were two animals because the second animal could have an even greater impact. When I was met with questioning looks, I explained that maybe the two animals would go out for dinner and a movie and a few months later they might have a baby animal that could be shared with a third family. They understood now. A life changer for the families and maybe the entire village.

Anyway, somebody said that we should really buy a goat. We should actually do this. I said, "Put your money where your mouth is." So they did.

I had one wired, working connection to the internet so we looked at heifer.org and found out that to have them send a goat to those who needed it, the cost would be $120. We also noticed some of the other options and costs for different, useful animals that they would send and the stories of successful impacts that had already been realized. My students were impressed that with such a seemingly small change, that the people they were reading about could overcome such daunting obstacles.

I started to collect money during that class hour. Two more classes of students came in and with little more than the explanation of what we started and the opportunity from me, students contributed $60. Half a goat! It was a good first day.

The next day students in each class brought in more money to contribute. We added another $22. And the third day, they contributed another $22. We were only $16 away from buying a goat. A flippant comment had led to real action, and we were really close to helping a family, a village, change their lives for the better.

Students in the school started talking about what we were doing. They all wanted to buy a goat, too. An administrator heard about what we were doing and stopped by to see how close we were to meeting our goal. He offered to kick in the rest. I had already planned to do that, if we didn't meet our goal by the last day before the break. I thought that one way or another *we were going to buy a goat.* Somebody was going to get us there. I thought either he will, or I will, or they will. I thought maybe we should all buy a goat.

Well, we bought a goat. A student came in before school on the morning of the last day before the winter break. He asked how much we had to go until we bought a goat. I told him we needed $16. He said, "I want to pay it off." I said, "Really, that's a lot of money?" He said, "I don't need it." He continued to say that he didn't want to do it in class because then everybody would be like "he's such a good guy and all that." He just wanted to do it to complete the mission and make sure some other people got what they needed. He wanted to help. No fanfare or pat on the back needed. He counted out and handed over sixteen dollars. Then he smiled, turned, and headed to his first hour class.

These people. These wonderful people bought a goat.

Those students were not always perfect, but when given the opportunity to help a family in a way they'll never see, they stepped up. Those who could afford it gave something to someone they've never met, and never will. They won't see the effect, but they have faith and hope that they are doing good in their little way. These students were helping a family and a village overcome obstacles and make a better life for themselves and maybe some others, too. What seemed like a simple failure to connect to the internet turned into something more important: a global connection.

Jason Bretzmann is an award-winning social studies teacher, innovation integrator, and national speaker from Wisconsin. He has delivered engaging and practical presentations throughout the United States and in Canada on personalized professional development, flipped learning, and effective educational technology use. He is co-author and publisher of Personalized PD: Flipping Your Professional Development and Flipping 2.0: Practical Strategies for Flipping Your Class. He is also the president and founder of The Bretzmann Group where he is a consultant on Stories in EDU, personalized PD, flipclass, and ed tech strategies. Jason has been learning with his students and encouraging innovation since the mid-'90s. Connect with him on Twitter @jbretzmann or via storiesinedu.com

CHAPTER 2: OVERCOMING OBSTACLES

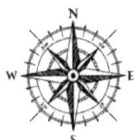

Sketchnotes In The Middle of Awful
by Sherrill Knezel

Brodie was a bright elementary art student with a quick and dry sense of humor. He liked to draw. Actually he *loved* to draw, and he was good at it. His solutions to our project problems in elementary art always pushed the limits of the assignments. As his art teacher, I had a constant answer to his frequent question, "Can I do it this way?" I'd reply "Why not?"

When I stumbled upon Mike Rohde's book, *Sketchnote Handbook* a couple of years ago, I was drawn into the world of visual notetaking and graphic recording. I had an immediate question: *WHY aren't we teaching students to do this?*

I knew that this technique of using a combination of words and images to make meaning and relevance from verbal or text-based information belonged in education. I began talking with anyone who would listen about how this valuable literacy tool could have infinite potential in schools. Almost immediately, I had become a sketchnote advocate.

By then, Brodie had moved onto middle school. It was just about two years after we initially met that Brodie's mom reached out to me. She had heard that I had been using this technique in my classes. She shared that Brodie had done well in elementary school but had struggled in middle school. He could memorize everything early on, but the amount of information had now exploded in 7th grade and he couldn't keep up. He had struggled with taking notes to help him study and remember.

The following year, Brodie was diagnosed with Dysgraphia, a learning disability that affects a student's written expression. Brodie could understand complex concepts and ideas, but translating them back onto the page in written form was difficult.

The question must have been in the back of my mind again: "Can I do it this way?"

Knowing that Brodie was a visual learner and that he enjoyed drawing, I met with his parents and explained why I thought visual note taking just might be the tool he needed to help him succeed now and as he moved onto high school. We got him started. Over the next two years, Brodie worked at taking great notes by sketchnoting. And these were not just notes. They were an effective tool that a bright student with a quick and dry sense of humor could use to organize his learning. Even more, they were a way for Brodie to regain control of his learning and find success again.

Over those years I received updates from Brodie's mom on his progress. I love that I still get emails from her sharing examples of just what a difference visual note taking has made for him.

When I ask Brodie how visual notes helped him, his quick response is, "Well, it definitely helped me pass Chemistry!"

Conventional methods weren't working for him and before using visual notes, he would try to write important information down, but in the end, he felt deflated. Brodie's parents advocated for him to be able to use visual notes in class, on homework and on tests, and his teachers saw the benefits, too, and agreed to give them a try. And they've worked.

For Brodie, being able to use visual notes allowed him to lean on his drawing skills and it has become, as he says, "a treat in the middle of awful" for him. He uses humor, makes it into a game, and challenges himself to draw the topic the teacher is covering. He describes it as a "back and forth with my mind." As he takes notes he continually asks himself where he can add a drawing. He uses his notes and the images immediately to help him recall what was said in class.

As he headed into his junior year in high school, I asked Brodie what advice he would give to teachers who were thinking about allowing or encouraging their students to use visual notes. "For me, they work better than traditional note taking. I would tell them they should try it. They have nothing to lose!"

When it comes to using visual notes in education, I agree with Brodie and I would add that there is everything to gain. Brodie is just one student, but for him, learning about and using this literacy tool was impactful and transformative. Imagine what an infinitely positive impact visual note taking could make if all students had this tool in their toolbox as an option to demonstrate understanding and create personal relevance and meaning if it works for them.

Since working with Brodie, he has used visual notes in his college scholarship applications. Who knows where he'll be able to apply this tool next. He and other students have inspired me to keep sharing the message. I have had the chance to work with college students in study skills classes, young men in juvenile detention, autistic students and adults, students with ADHD, and educators across levels and content areas around visual notes. I believe that drawing *is* thinking and we owe it to our students to enable and empower them to communicate visually in our changing world.

When we open up doors and possibilities for students to convey their learning in a way that makes sense to them, we empower those students to take control of their learning and overcome their obstacles.

"Can I do it this way?" I continue to reply, "Why not?" And I plan to continue answering that way while I help spread the option of sketchnoting around the world.

Sherrill Knezel *is a K-12 art educator and graphic recorder in the Wauwatosa (WI) School District since 1992. She leads PD on visual literacy/visual note taking in school districts and community organizations as a means to enhance communication, clarity, and collaboration. Sherrill uses graphic recording to support local and national organizations doing work around education, equity, inclusion, and social justice. Her mission is to share visual note taking as a powerful literacy tool with the world.*

CHAPTER 3: OVERCOMING OBSTACLES

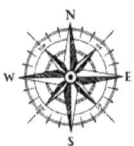

Purpose Combats Complacency
by Julie Fishburn

It occurred to me several years ago that I had become very comfortable in my career. I was a veteran teacher of over twenty years. I knew "the ropes" and was well-equipped to train others along the way. My lesson plans were done. Done. My tests were done. Done. Checked both of those off my list a long time ago. Sure, I added a lesson here and there as I saw fit, but other than that, I was on cruise-control. Life was good. Work was work and rarely came home with me. That was always one of my golden rules as I passed my second and third year of teaching. Respect your time!

Then a peculiar thing happened. I became unhappy. I was bored. I was too far away from retirement to just ride it out until then. And when I really thought about it, I didn't want to ride it out. I hadn't been completely stagnant. Things had evolved after all. I wasn't receiving messages in print in a mailbox down in the office anymore. A mailbox that had to be checked a few times a day to ensure nothing was missed and was frequently bursting with stuff. Now, those once in-print messages were streaming through my endless e-mail inbox. So, things had evolved. But email alone couldn't be the only progress I had made in all these years of teaching, could it? I had managed to become stale in my career doing the same projects as the year before and the year before that, for no other reason than that's what I had always done.

I had hosted several student teachers and the experience was something I enjoyed. These new teachers were bright and full of energy. And ideas.

They were far from the old loaf of stale bread forgotten in the cabinet. These student teachers weren't even bread yet, they were still dough that needed to be shaped into... anything. Some of them went on to be bread while others were pastries or croissants. The type of bread is really irrelevant, what's important is the process they go through to find the proper shelf for their professional self. It's the process by which one learns and becomes acclimated to the education profession that is important. It's the stamina needed to enjoy a fulfilling and rewarding career. They were each a breath of fresh air and their excitement was contagious. But they weren't fully ready yet. Maybe I wasn't either.

A change was coming, but I had no warning for where it would start. For me, I realized my quest as a teacher wasn't to achieve cruise-control status. I wanted to evolve with education and regain the excitement that the doughy, student teachers exuded. *That* became my quest—my new mission as a teacher. And it would leave what most teachers desire as their legacy. Teachers want to leave a lasting impression on their students while preparing them for the next chapter in their lives. How far away do we get from the core reason we became a teacher in the first place? Hopefully not *too* far.

My new quest began with a student teacher asking me, no...*challenging* me with: "Do you know what a flipped classroom is?" Of course, I know what a flipped classroom is! How insulting! I've never been one to pretend I know something when I don't, but for some reason this time I did. It alarmed me. I had heard the term flipped classroom, but did I have a working knowledge of what this concept was? No. No, I didn't. The truth was that I hadn't the slightest idea what a flipped classroom was. But one thing was for certain. I was going to find out.

I have always liked learning. I already held a Master's Degrees in Curriculum and Instruction and another one in Special Education. I enjoyed being a lifelong learner, but somewhere along the way I began to slip, assuming that my student teacher had more to learn from me than I from him. Seriously, what the heck was my purpose? When I was his age, why did I choose education as a career field? Could I remember? I wanted to make connections with students and see them succeed in life. To encourage them during struggles, support them, and relish in their successes, too. Yes, of course I could remember this, but how much in touch was I with that purpose today?

Being really in touch with that purpose means being cognizant of it every day, reflecting upon it and striving to reach out and collaborate with other educators. I was aware of my purpose, but did I call it to mind daily? Maybe I did weekly, but was that enough? I really want students to learn. I want to see those lightbulb moments students have when it clicks for them. My students were performing well on tests and homework. They were good little point-collectors, but could I really claim that they had acquired new knowledge? How much of it was I seeing? When I really assessed my daily classroom interactions, the answer was "not much." But my world was about to experience a paradigm shift.

As with any issue, problem, or action, it is almost impossible to be aware of it and ignore it. It's like when you're at the dinner table and someone slurps their water or scrapes their teeth across their fork. I am now aware and every time I hear a slurp or a scrape, the hairs stand up on the back of my neck. Just ignore it? I *can't*!

Now that I was aware that my purpose in the classroom had slipped away from me, it was completely impossible to ignore or put it on the back burner until I had time for it. Let's face it. Time is something that is not on our side. We never have enough time. If I put it off until I have time, I may never get around to the basics by reconnecting with my purpose in the classroom. The purpose that drove me to class each week at the university. The one that allowed me to subject myself to the uncomfortableness of my practicum hours or stressfulness of student teaching.

The state of my teacher existence needed some serious help. But, where would I even start? There was one thing I was already pretty good at: talking. I wasn't the most outgoing teenager myself. In fact, I was the one in the back of the class avoiding eye contact with the teacher at all costs. So, how did I end up being a "sage on the stage?"

I distinctly remember the first lesson I taught. It was one of the most frightening and awkward experiences of my college career. Getting up in front of anyone and speaking was a terrifying experience. Still, I pressed on. Subjecting myself to this sort of torture became routine and over time I had managed to turn this weakness into a strength. I became a pretty good storyteller! In my complacency, though, I had forgotten that about myself. I had conquered that fear and I was a better teacher for it.

Now, that I had remembered how uncomfortable it was to push the limits of my comfort zone, I had this odd desire to try it again. Before I could do that, though, I still had to find someone to fill me in on this whole flipped classroom concept. Most educators are great sharers. All I did was ask around and I found someone well-versed in the flipped classroom.

This was probably one of the biggest lessons I learned on my journey. Collaboration can be very powerful, but it's not just sharing lessons. It's sharing knowledge, asking for ideas, advice and clarification. It's a partnership of two or more educators sharing growth, a friendship, and a journey. It's connecting and networking with other teachers, administrators, counselors, instructional resource teachers, instructional technology teachers, college professors, superintendents, or anyone in education. Great ideas can be generated by having conversations with others. I challenged myself to connect with those within my building and outside of my building.

In fact, the teacher I found to help me understand the flipped classroom was actually from another high school in our district and of a different content area. What I learned was twofold: 1) flipped classroom was a lot about technology, and 2) collaboration can be very beneficial even with teachers outside of your content area. The first part of my lesson really bothered me and the second part was really a by-product of my whole journey. I didn't understand technology, and I wasn't sure I really wanted to. I took typing class, and computers didn't make it into the classroom until I was a high school sophomore. Here I was again with something that made my skin crawl. And again I accepted the challenge.

Collaboration became the key in my professional growth as it related to my personal quest to learn technology. This was something that I was driven to do, and I did not wait for it to arrive at my school. I went and got it. I began to seek out those connections that could help me along the way to navigate these unfamiliar waters. The other high school teacher I connected with from a neighboring high school had really given me a wealth of materials to start my own flipped classroom, and my students were really enjoying it. Even though they weren't like me because they had grown up immersed in technology, I was now speaking their language.

It was a significant change in my classroom. I was now the "guide on the side." I was once again able to build more meaningful relationships. Being a semester class teacher, it was not uncommon for me to have almost 300 students in a single school year. That's a lot! The flipped classroom revitalized my class! I was able to guide students through the learning process by having conversations with each of them. I didn't have time for that before because my old self had a curriculum to get through. I had missed this relationship-building and really enjoyed this aspect of our new process.

The final major component of my journey was my personal learning network. My new friend had suggested that I join Twitter. Um, scary. Again. But I approached it the way I did the flipped classroom challenge. Baby steps. I've shared a lot of ideas, gained a ton of insight, and met a lot of great people along the way. It wasn't long before I was moderating Twitter chats and presenting on various topics at the local level and the FlipCon Kansas conference. I even started facilitating a specialized professional learning community on the flipped class in my own building.

All of those weaknesses—public speaking, technology, collaboration, Twitter—became my strengths. It revolutionized my classroom, my students' experiences and my role as an educator. That journey, the one that was very uncomfortable at times, brought me right back to my purpose, which was definitely *not* complacency.

That purpose is at the very core of the fire that burns inside each educator and drives them to come to school each day with the hope of facilitating student success. The fire that drags us out of bed after a sleepless night, so that we may connect with 30 smiling, or maybe frowning faces. To lose that fire, that purpose, is to become stagnant in your career. If one begins to lose, or has lost the reason for which one becomes a teacher in the first place, then reconnecting or re-inventing is the remedy.

Let's face it: those of us who entered education for the wrong reasons—summers off, no weekends, 40-hour work weeks—are long gone. They only lasted a year or two before leaving the education profession for another. We are already here for the "right" reasons and deciding to re-invent our goals as an educator, or reconnecting with a lost goal, is entirely an individual decision. And we should each choose to make it.

For me, it was a little of both. I've come to the realization that one of the best ways to combat complacency and burnout is lifelong learning through personalized professional development. And, so, my story has begun.

***Julie Fishburn** has been a teacher for over twenty years and serves as the social studies department chair in a high school centered around technology and project-based learning outside of Kansas City. Driven by a growth mindset, she is a continual learner and holds master's degrees in curriculum & instruction and special education. When not teaching, Julie enjoys presenting professional development in her building and across the district as well as at various conferences. She enjoys spending time with family and being outdoors.*

CHAPTER 4: OVERCOMING OBSTACLES

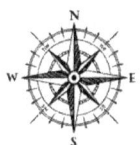

Intentional Decisions To Avoid Being The Obstacle

by Rachelle Dene Poth

A few years ago, it seemed as though motivation was lacking and students were not as engaged in the lessons as I had hoped. I was really struggling to keep my students engaged in the lessons and worse, I also noticed a decrease in student grades. I saw and could feel a significant decrease in student motivation and engagement. The focus had shifted to "why do we have to do this," and I could see that I was losing the attention of some students.

So I knew that I had to do things differently, think creatively, and take some risks. I wanted to keep us all moving forward, being excited for learning and to help each other achieve our best. I had reached out to my Professional Learning Network (PLN) through the Voxer app for some ideas and to share experiences. It proved to be very helpful to have these conversations. However, nobody could really figure out what the issue was. *Why were the students not engaged, what was I doing wrong, and what could I be doing better?*

I took it as an opportunity to try new things and to offer more student choice and flexibility in my classroom. At first, I tried to offer more choices in what students were doing and provided opportunities for them to be part of the decisions made about what we were doing in the classroom. I found some success there, but didn't get all that I had hoped for with this change.

I decided that I just had to dive in and make some big changes. This of course was a great risk because I really did not know where to start. I worried that things wouldn't go as I had planned. I had concerns that perhaps the students would take it as a way to not work as hard or worse, their learning potential would be diminished in some way. I worried that in making changes I would negatively impact their learning. However, I remained hopeful that by giving them more choices and by being more flexible with my planning, students would begin to drive their own learning.

My goal was to promote more peer collaboration, with my facilitation of their learning and the creation of some diverse learning experiences. Some of the ideas that I had in mind and tried were to create small groups of students and offer different choices in the types of activities that they could work on during class. By doing this, it gave me the opportunity to move around the classroom rather than being stuck at the front of the room talking for the entire period. But more importantly it gave students an opportunity to collaborate with their peers and work on their social emotional learning skills while interacting with the content in a more authentic way. Sometimes I would ask students to come up with their own ways to practice the vocabulary or the grammar topics for example, and other times I would create a choice board in which students had nine different activities to select from and could decide how they wanted to work with the content on those days.

These different learning methods led to a lot of positives in the classroom. Students were building relationships with their peers and I was able to work with each student on a more personal level and provide feedback right when they needed it. I hoped that my students would sustain motivation and engagement through to the end of the year. I had to remove obstacles to allow those things to happen.

The first big obstacle I decided was the rows of desks in my classroom. For weeks, I kept looking at my room and the design. During class, I noticed that if I was teaching and a student asked a question that I would lose the attention of most of the class to respond to that one student. Then I'd have to re-engage the students, which of course resulted in a loss of valuable instructional time. The desks were an obstacle to students being able to stay engaged, to participate, to collaborate, and even to hear the responses of their peers. I thought about how much time our students spend sitting in rows, passively learning, simply facing the front of the room, with only a few opportunities to move around and interact with their peers bothered me tremendously.

I had enough of the stringent structure of our teacher-centered classroom, and so at 9:37 on a morning in September, I shifted the desks around the room, without any idea whatsoever for a pattern. They are not the smallest desks and so it does limit what I can do, but it did not stop me. I moved the desks into random small groups and clusters around my room. My first obstacle was removed. In the beginning, it was a strange feeling to the students and me. When they entered the room that day, and looked for their assigned seat, they instead found a room in complete disarray. The shock on their faces was priceless.

Change one was a success. The students liked the opportunity to sit with their friends, and to be grouped differently each week. They liked being able to work more with and learn from their peers. They liked learning *about* their peers as well.

To promote peer collaboration and the building of relationships, we would work in small groups on the same activity or move around through different learning stations. When I decided to try station rotations in my class, I randomly grouped students and created four or five different learning stations in the classroom. I tried to vary the activities so that some involved nothing more than students creating flash cards or working on a worksheet, others would be watching an interactive video, or using a game-based learning tool. The students looked at the materials and got themselves started, it did not take long for them to keep each other engaged in the activities and it was great for me to be able to move around and work with each group or each student as needed throughout the class.

All of this was a huge risk for me, and definitely felt uncomfortable at first, because I was breaking traditional classroom structures. But by doing this, it instead opened up the classroom more to flexible learning and flexible spaces. It engaged students who had not been nearly as engaged before. Students were coming in to tell me how much more they were enjoying class and learning more, being able to have time both to interact with peers and have individualized instruction. Hearing this, I knew that the risk had been worth it. The removal of the confining and isolating rows had opened up a new way of learning for my students and me.

The second obstacle was that I was the only one doing the talking for the majority of the class. I was teaching as I had been taught, deciding both everything about the lesson, and how students would show their learning. For years, I gave little in the form of choices in how to show what they learned. It occurred to me after reviewing some student projects that I was not promoting student choice very much. I was giving the information and then simply asking students to create basically the same thing that I had given them, in the way that I wanted. For example I was creating the rubric and determining the format their project had to take when I could have been providing multiple options and ways for them to meet the requirements of the rubric. And even better, I could have simply told students the type of content that I wanted to be included in their work and let them decide the best way to demonstrate their learning.

To change this I decided to get out of the way. I started by taking some digital tools and teaching students lesson with them, and providing a short overview of how each tool was used. After the very brief overview, I placed these tools and the choices about what to use in the hands of the students. I wanted them to create their own lessons or design assessments. I wanted them to lead our class.

I hoped to achieve my goal that the students would become more engaged in learning. I wanted them to develop their creativity, enjoy this role reversal, and have fun becoming the teacher in the classroom. As for me, I wanted to gain the additional perspective by becoming a student in the classroom. Even though it was a bit of a risk, and I was opening myself up to a lot of questions, I was also quite hopeful that the experience would be a positive learning experience for all students. Ideally, by having that freedom of choice, students would become empowered and drive their own learning.

My goal was for them to transform from being consumers in the classroom to emerge as creators who would take more control in their learning. To go from simply the learners being talked to or talked at, to leaders of their own learning. What I wanted was to move from having learners to having leaders, and create more student empowerment in the classroom. I needed to get out of their way and let them lead.

In order to grow, we need to reflect in our practice daily. Reflection is so important. I value the feedback from students as part of my reflective practice, and I try to have conversations or create short surveys for students to complete so I can understand what they really think about the changes I have made in class. I provide a safe and comfortable way for them to share their ideas with me, because I have found over the years that sometimes students are more open when they have the chance to respond in an anonymous survey, rather than have a direct face-to-face conversation.

As educators, we are lifelong learners and we are not immune to making mistakes. We have to be the risk-takers and continue to evolve in our practice. Sometimes things go as we hoped and sometimes they do not, but these are not lost opportunities. If we continue to do the same that we have always done, there is no opportunity for growth, no opportunity for the experience of setting goals, and no opportunities to face challenges, share failures, or celebrate successes. We need to do this and *model* it for our students.

Perhaps we should all look around our learning spaces. What are the obstacles? Could it be something as simple as the classroom layout that is limiting peer collaboration and the building of relationships? Or is it the teacher, standing in the front of the room, leading each day and not opening up enough opportunities for the students to take the lead, changing the classroom from teacher-centered to student-centered and student-driven?

At the end of each year I ask students for some feedback, usually through a survey or a video response tool. I review their responses over my summer as a way to reflect on the previous year and also to plan for the upcoming year. But after removing the big obstacles, the feedback was different. Only after a few weeks of changing things in our classroom, I started to have students come in and tell me what a difference it was making for them. These were students who did not engage as much in class in the year prior, or students who at times I would have to get their attention back into the class. The students were coming to tell me what they liked about class...and doing so on their own.

I also noticed the relationships developing among the students. Several of them commented throughout the year that they felt like they had their own family in the classroom, that it was a very welcoming environment, and that they felt comfortable being in there and working with their peers. Besides hearing from them, it was something that I could see as well. By removing myself as the center of the classroom and moving around the classroom instead, it created a much better environment for learning and growing together.

Every classroom has obstacles. Let's all take a look around and see what is preventing us and our students from being the best that we can be. What obstacles are preventing the most engaging, authentic learning experiences that we could create? Let's start there and see where we can go with our students. It's okay to be wrong and to make mistakes. It's *not* okay to envision a better way and refuse to make changes when we realize this. I am a work in progress and a constant learner. And I'll continue to proceed in that way.

Rachelle Dene Poth *teaches Spanish and a STEAM course called What's nExT? In Emerging Technology. She is also an attorney and has a master's degree in instructional technology. Rachelle serves as president for the ISTE Teacher Education Network and communications chair for the Mobile Learning Network. She was selected as one of the "20 To Watch" by the NSBA and awared the PAECT Outstanding Teacher of the Year for 2017. She is a future-ready instructional coach for 2018 and a Microsoft innovative educator expert for 2018-19. She is an author and regular blogger for* Getting Smart *and* Kidblog.

CHAPTER 5: OVERCOMING OBSTACLES

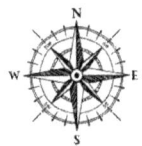

We Are On This Journey Together

by Dennis Griffin, Jr.

I strive to empower students in order to change the trajectory of their future outcomes. In order to empower anyone, you must believe in them. It takes both empowerment and belief. Imagine swinging at a baseball with an imaginary bat. All the belief in the world won't hit that ball. It takes the empowerment of a strong bat. Conversely, a strong bat that never leaves your shoulder will have no results. Belief must be present so the batter will take the mighty swing. I make sure I equip my students with the tools to swing for the fences.

When I was a classroom mathematics teacher, I had the opportunity to serve my last class of students for two consecutive years. My classroom was very diverse and many of my students often lacked the confidence to see themselves as mathematicians. A few of my students expressed that they had not experienced success for a number of years, and I was determined to change that. Many had started to believe that math was difficult, that they were in the "low group", and that the stereotypes people had placed on them were true.

My moral imperative reinforced my belief that I would empower my students' abilities to overcome obstacles. For me, school served a greater role than the content I was teaching. My job was to prepare my students to serve and participate in a democratic society, thus proving the skeptics wrong in regard to their predetermined outcomes.

I remember one young lady who was transferred to my math class. She told me she hated math, she was never going to be good at it, and had no desire to participate in class or complete any of her assignments. When I attempted to redirect this young lady, she told me that she was not scared of me like these other kids. I shared with her that she had no reason to be afraid of me. I explained, "I care about you as a person and our classroom is built upon respect for one another." I saw the potential inside of her, but she didn't seem to.

Rather than unleash her talent, she would have outbursts and attempt to disrupt the class. She hoped that I would have her removed from class. But I didn't. She shared with me that I was not like her other teachers, because the other teachers would have kicked her out of class by now. I smiled and said, "I never kick kids out of my class. It is my job to make sure you learn, and I cannot do that if you are not here. You are a part of my school community, and I am responsible for your future. I have to make sure you are ready for college. I will never give up!" She replied, "Mr. Griffin, I do not like school now, and I will never go to college." I smiled and said, "We will see."

She had a difficult time adjusting, and it made perfectly good sense. She was the only student that was removed from her class. She felt that she was the outsider. Not to mention math was not her favorite subject. After the first month of school, we came to an understanding and I started to see the changes within her.

To help form relationships I was present outside before school, in the hallways before the bell rang, during lunch, and after school. I took the time to know what television shows and music were popular. My relationship-building was tested when I had to tell my newest student that she had to serve an after-school detention with me. She made sure to tell everyone that she was not going to show up for it. I smiled and said that I expected to see her at my door at the end of the day. I promised her that I was not going to come looking for her either.

When the bell rang at the end of the day, she was there. As she walked in she had an attitude, and I asked her to try entering the classroom again. When she entered again, I told her she was dismissed. She became wide-eyed in disbelief. I told her that I appreciated that she was on time. I asked her to think about what we can do to ensure her success in my class and her others. The condition was that if we had to have this conversation again within seven days, she'd owe me for this time as well. She agreed and left with a huge smile. I was the first teacher to give her a second chance.

The next day, I noticed the transformation beginning. When the students were working on their problems and anticipating going to the board, she slowly raised her hand. She asked me a question and we talked through the problem. When it was time to call on someone to go to the board, she slowly raised her hand again. She explained her problem and the solution was incorrect. In a very excited voice, I thanked her for giving me her best effort and gave her a high five. The class followed by applauding for her. Our mantra was that mistakes were how we learned. She was validated and was beginning to be a part of something that was greater than herself. The next thing I knew, she was an active participant and could not keep her hand down.

Even so, she would often tell me that I was doing too much by having high expectations for her and the quality of her work. I emphasized that there were no shortcuts. She voiced these ideas the week prior to spring break by saying, "Mr. Griffin, you know you are like the only teacher in the building teaching, right? Everyone else is watching movies and having fun." I know she didn't mean this literally, but I reminded her that I was preparing her for her future and added, "I do not have a second to waste."

Something I did or something I said must have clicked with this young lady. Or maybe she did learn to love math, or at least not hate it. But most likely it was that she had my constant reminders, my never-ending re-focus, and a relentless advocate for her current and future success. She had someone on her side who would never give up on her, and she responded to my high expectations. After two years together, she made sure that I was the first person she took a picture with at the 8th Grade Celebration. Four years after that important photo, I had become a principal and she had embarked on a successful high school experience.

At the end of those four years, my former student tracked me down again, reaching out in three different ways. She tried social media, email, *and* my office phone. My secretary delivered a phone message from her and said she sounded very professional. It is important for me to note that I had not interacted with her in four years.

I called back and she said to me, "Mr. Griffin, I want to say thank you for never giving up on me. I wanted to let you know that I am graduating from high school this year and I am going to college." Not only did she get accepted to three colleges, she even received a scholarship. I heard her mom saying "Thank you" in the background. I reminded her mom, "I promised you back then that we will always be connected and that we are on this journey together. Thank you for entrusting your daughter's education to me." My former student then said, "Mr. Griffin, my graduation is a big moment in my life, and I wanted to invite you to attend because you played a major role in my life. I wanted you to share this moment with me."

I attended her graduation and was able to stand at the entrance of the processional as my former students walked in. I saw their faces light up as we made eye contact. At the end of the graduation, I had the opportunity to see many of the students that I taught. I embraced them and their parents. When the young lady found me she was smiling from ear to ear, and told me that I was still doing too much. She said she would not be who she is today if it were not for me.

Every year, I take the time to reflect about my former students and contemplate how they are progressing. I reflect on our classroom and the lessons we learned together. The number one lesson my students taught me was to have an unwavering belief in their potential and their futures. Belief plants the seed. We have to believe in our students and wait and watch as they grow into who they were meant to be.

In our world, we have become so obsessed with immediate gratification that we have associated delayed gratification with a lack of progress. In the world of education, the fruits of our labor may not manifest for ten or fifteen years. In the interim, as educators, we must believe that our actions will empower our students to persevere in the face of adversity as they strive to become productive members of our democratic society. The task that we are charged with is not easy nor is it for the faint of heart. I am a teacher of students, not a teacher of content. I believe with all of my heart that serving our students is worth it. And I'll never give up.

Dennis Griffin Jr. *serves as the principal of Prairie Elementary School in Waukesha, WI. He has seven years of experience as a middle school educator and is entering his fifth year as an administrator. He is currently pursuing his doctoral studies in educational leadership.*

CHAPTER 6: RELATIONSHIPS

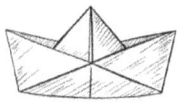

FFA and High Expectations
by Dr. Robin Mclean

In 1987, I was a shy middle school student. My agriculture teacher had encouraged me to go to FFA* Camp Oswegatchie in New York's Adirondack mountains for a week in the summer. The cabins and the campsites had no electricity, so conditions were rustic. It was nearly seven hours from home. It was a lot to consider for a shy middle school student. I went anyway. It rained most of the week, and I remember spilling an entire bowl of salsa on my lap one day at lunch. At the end-of-the-week dance, I found a chair to curl up in and sleep. Camp was clearly not my thing, and I vowed to myself never to return to FFA camp. The fates, however, conspired against me and somehow I won "Camper of the Week." The unexpected award earned me a free week at camp the following summer. I guess I had to go back.

Following that first summer, I returned to Camp Oswegatchie for four more summers as a camper. In addition, our teacher brought us to camp for long weekends in the winter. Eventually I got a job there, and I worked a summer as an assistant camp cook (something many of my current friends find amusing as they know I am a disaster in the kitchen). I returned for another summer as the Leadership Training Coordinator to teach leadership classes at the camp, as well as coordinate leadership contests.

Following my time at camp, I finished college, moved from New York to New Jersey to take a job teaching high school, worked for the state of New Jersey, and then returned to the classroom as a middle school agricultural science teacher. I've come a long way from that shy middle school student. Sometimes I wonder what impact the relationships I built at camp have had on my future as an educator.

Part of teaching agricultural science goes beyond classroom instruction and includes serving as an FFA advisor. This allows me to foster and develop some unique relationships with my students that would not happen if I were a teacher that only saw these students in a classroom setting. Through community service activities, we clean up roadsides and assist a local fire company in their chicken BBQ. This allows students to see me as a "real" person in jeans and a baseball cap. If it's early enough on a weekend morning, they also see me as a coffee-guzzling fiend. With the multitude of career development events and contests we prepare for, and the leadership roles students assume in conducting FFA chapter activities, they see me as a coach and a motivator. As one student said "You're so cool and fun at FFA events, but you have high expectations of us in the classroom." I don't take that as a slight on my teaching, as I believe in setting the bar high and helping students reach it. Rather it's an observation of the different type of relationship I am able to have with students actively involved in FFA activities beyond the school day.

My first year teaching in a middle school classroom started in 2007—twenty years after my first summer at Camp Oswegatchie. As I learned about my students and their interests, my own experiences at Camp Oswegatchie came to mind. This was a group of youth who I thought might enjoy and could benefit from this camp experience. I reached out to Camp Oswegatchie to get information about their current summer camp program. I learned all of the steps that were required to get school approval. I shared about camp with students and their parents. Then, the adventure began. Like me, some of my students have chosen to experience the adventure of FFA not only beyond the school day, but beyond the border of their state by going to Camp Oswegatchie.

The adventure continues for my students and for me even today. Bringing students to FFA camp allows me to not just build relationships with my students in a non-traditional setting, but also develop relationships with their parents that go beyond traditional school communication. After all, I am going to be taking their child over seven hours away from them for five days with no cell phone and no internet. For some students, this is their first time away from home. It is very important that the parents know they can trust me and that they clearly know what the camp experience will be like for their child. As technology has improved, I have made sure that during the first few days of camp I take a picture of each student engaged in an activity and when I do the midweek trip to town where there is phone service, I send a picture of their child to each parent.

Taking students to a summer camp hundreds of miles from home is quite the adventure. Imagine being up at 4:00 a.m. on a Saturday morning in the summer so you can load a van full of middle school students to take them on a seven plus hour ride. My first trip, I thought there would be sleeping most of that ride. Wrong! They were awake, chatting, singing, and creating a general cacophony of noise. No statements of "The trip will go faster if you sleep," could quiet them.

On that trip to camp, though, I got to know my students much better than I previously had. I heard about what their summer adventures had been, how they were (or weren't) progressing on their summer assignments, what they were starting to think about as their career goals, and other aspects of their lives. Before arriving at camp, we stopped for lunch where we learned the life skill of tipping a waiter or waitress. It was an adventure in math and a surprise for some of them. When we finally arrived at camp, camp staff essentially became responsible for my students. However, I let them know where I would be seated at meal times and encouraged them to check in with me.

While at FFA camp, I had the opportunity to see my students flourish in a setting that they are not usually in. They challenged themselves on high ropes courses and climbing walls. Being the only school there from New Jersey, they met new people and developed friendships. They survived and thrived away from home at their evening campsites where there is no electricity, just flashlights and campfires. At meal time, they would stop by my table to tell me what they did or where they were going to be and ask if I would be coming to watch them. They made me tie-dyed t-shirts and friendship bracelets. They stepped out of their comfort zones and generally blossomed.

At the end of the week, we got back in the van and headed south so I could return them to their homes. The ride back was a jumble of noise for about the first hour and then sleep caught up with them. An informal survey revealed that most wanted to go back again the next summer and it *had* to be during Week 5. Week 5 was the week we attended the first summer we went simply because it fit into my schedule. However, my students had formed relationships with other campers who always go to Oswegatchie Week 5. To them the thought of any other week seemed ridiculous. As the campers I took in middle school left me for high school, some continued to go to FFA camp. Since we are in the same school district, this was easily accomplished.

FFA Camp doesn't just give me a chance to develop relationships with my students. Since we are there with other schools, it provides me an opportunity to spend the week with other teachers that come from diverse backgrounds. Although it is an FFA camp and the majority of the teachers there are agriculture teachers, some of the teachers chaperoning are technology teachers, art teachers, science teachers or other educators. As we work and dine together during the week, we get to learn from each other. Those relationships and dialogues carry on beyond camp through social media and email. This summer after camp, the hunter safety instructor will be joining my significant other and me on a Mediterranean cruise. Just as students develop long lasting relationships through their camp experience, I do as well.

When I was a camper, I would mail letters to the friends I made when I was at Camp Oswegatchie. We would see each other at New York FFA events. Today, some of us are still in touch. For my FFA members that went to camp, they have a different way of keeping in touch. They communicate via Facebook, Instagram, and Snapchat. Who knows what communication tools they'll be able to use in the future. Since we are in two different states and their FFA paths don't otherwise cross, they have actually worked out mini-vacations and get-togethers with each other either at each other's homes or at a common meeting point that their parents approve of. This is one of the greatest gifts I get from FFA Camp—watching my students form relationships that help enrich their lives.

Keeping in touch is not only for my students and their friends, but also for me and some of these students as they graduate and move on. The time spent on the way to and from Camp Oswegatchie, as well as at camp, has allowed me to foster stronger relationships with some of my students than I might have otherwise. A young lady who went to FFA Camp with me as a 7th grader and attended five weeks of camp, recently graduated college and is now an educator herself. We have attended Edcamps and Project Learning Tree trainings together. Two other long term campers who are 2018 graduates, aspire to become agriculture teachers, so I feel confident they will continue to be a part of my life.

I do not get paid to take my students to FFA Camp. I take them because I know the impact FFA Camp Oswegatchie had on me as a student. I take them because I want to share with them the wonder of a camp in the Adirondacks, to help them challenge themselves, to watch them grow, to see them build relationships, and to get to know them better. When we are back in school, I can continue to build on the strengths I have seen. I take them because, for some, it is the first time away from home, and I want them to be exposed to travel and the adventure it brings. I take them because I can learn from them as I watch and listen to their experiences. I take them because it is a unique adventure that might help change their lives in ways similar to the way it helped change mine.

*The National FFA Organization is an organization for students enrolled in agricultural education classes with the mission of developing premier leadership, personal growth, and career success. Until 1988, it was known as the Future Farmers of America. However, the name changed to reflect the diversity of the careers available in the food, agriculture, and natural resources industry.

Robin C. McLean *is an agricultural science teacher from New Jersey. She has over twenty years of experience in the classroom and state educational planning. She earned her BS from Cornell University, her MS from Virginia Tech, and her Ed.D. from Rowan University. Dr. McLean has a passion for opening her students' eyes to the world around them and helping develop agriculturally literate consumers. When she's not teaching, she enjoys foreign travel and Broadway shows.*

CHAPTER 7: RELATIONSHIPS

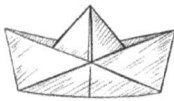

Tiny Ripples of Hope Build a Current
by Kris Jenkins

I'll never forget the day that the black car with the two men in full Air Force dress uniforms knocked on the door of our tiny duplex in Lincoln, Nebraska, before school on September 20th, 1968.

When I was seven years old, my father was killed in Vietnam. He was returning from a routine flight in a fighter jet and crashed just three miles short of the runway. No one can explain the crash or why he was even flying that plane. You see, he was trained to fly the largest planes, the B-52 bombers. Why he was flying a jet is still a mystery. His plane was not shot down, nor did he report any mechanical difficulties. It just went down. My father was pinned beneath the wreckage and it was said that he died instantly. The news of my father's death was so devastating that after the two men left, I remember sitting on my mom's lap with my younger brother and just crying our hearts out.

Later that week, we had to fly to Long Island, New York, because that's where my dad was raised and where the family burial plot was. His mother did not want him buried in Arlington. She wanted him closer to home, as he was her only child. I remember staying at my grandparents' house with a family member during the church service because my mom thought it was best that my brother and I not go. After the church service, we were picked up and taken to the graveside service.

Upon returning home, I was so afraid that something would happen to my mom. I didn't want to go to school. I screamed and cried under the dining room table. I didn't want to go to school. The logic of a seven-year old: My dad died when I was in school, so maybe my mom would, too. We were at an impasse.

My life was forever changed by caring educators. Two women for whom I will never be able to repay my debt—Louise Shuman and Maxine Moore, the elementary school counselor and my second grade teacher, respectively.

At school each morning, my mom would drop my younger brother and me off at the designated door. One of these ladies would be there waiting for us every day. I remember spending time in Mrs. Shuman's office, coloring and talking. Mrs. Shuman's office provided me a quiet place, a place where I could come to school and feel safe. A place where someone would sit and listen to me, my thoughts, my worries. Who I remember most though is Mrs. Moore.

Mrs. Moore would allow me to come into her classroom each morning before the rest of my classmates to do odd jobs for her. I sharpened pencils, passed out papers, and did other small jobs like that. These are things she would have normally done herself, but she saved them for me. We would talk which allowed me to feel comfortable in the classroom before the rest of my classmates arrived. Her compassion, caring, and understanding were game-changers for this scared little second-grader. You would have thought the story ended there, but it did not.

The next year my mom remarried and we moved to a farm a couple of hours away from Lincoln. Even though we lived in a different city, we still kept the same dentist back in Lincoln. Every time we'd go to the dentist, we'd meet up with Mrs. Moore to have an after-school snack. Secretly, my mom and Mrs. Moore worked together to make this happen. Because Mrs. Moore cared that much, she wanted to stay in touch with my family and me. I never lost the connection that Mrs. Moore and I had built over the years. While Mrs. Moore was the one to help me through the difficult early years, there were other kind-hearted educators along the way who focused on building relationships. They also helped me feel safe and cared for at school.

One highly influential teacher was Mr. Larry Fletcher, who taught high school English. Mr. Fletcher taught me that learning can be fun. While he cared about the content we were learning, he understood that the relationships that we formed in the classroom made everyone feel more comfortable. For example, each week, we'd play "Password" with our spelling words. One student would give a clue and their teammate would have to guess and spell the word. When we played the password game, Mr. Fletcher allowed the class to choose their own teams. Our favorite teams were when we competed boys against girls. For the record, the girls always won! The overly-competitive boys could never figure out how. Here is our secret: we all knew sign language. My mom was a speech pathologist and one of her students was deaf. She taught him and me sign language, which I, in turn, taught to all of my female friends. It didn't matter who was in the seat for "Password," because we all knew sign language and could communicate the correct answer every time.

The way we felt in Mr. Fletcher's classroom made everyone feel safe, respected and ready to learn. In the rural farming community where I grew up, class sizes were small. One section of English met during band, so all of the band kids had English together. Between the activities that Mr. Fletcher set up for us, and our connections through music, we developed such meaningful relationships with our classmates and teachers.

As I continued my education other influential educators would come into my life. Mrs. Diane Knutson and Mrs. Colleen Norvell (now Sipich) taught me the value of music. Going to music contest was the highlight of my high school years. It probably would have been easier to stay at our own school and listen to music, but instead Mrs. Knutson and Mrs. Norvell found unique experiences for us to bond with our classmates and grow in both our relationships and love for music. We listened to so many talented musicians on those trips, and my passion for music went to a new level. I have lifelong friendships that were formed from meeting students from other schools because we have bonded over our shared love of music. I still love to sing and play the piano, and I thank these two teachers for fostering a life-long passion for music inside me.

Another educator's passion for teaching and learning helped prepare me for my future. Mrs. Fran Conneally was the "Queen of Handouts." She was forever copying news articles for us to discuss in class. She was the only teacher I ever had in high school that asked us to do a research paper, complete with sources and a bibliography. I am so thankful for her passion and her leadership. I'm pretty sure I would never have survived college without all that I learned from her.

After high school, I returned to Lincoln for college. One of the first teachers to influence my young life in a positive way continued to impact me for my future. Mrs. Moore, my second grade teacher, wrote one of my reference letters for acceptance into the University of Nebraska-Lincoln. Because of her amazing influence and compassion, I, too, decided that I wanted to be a teacher. I had a double major in elementary education and early childhood education with a minor in music education. Many evenings you could find me at Mrs. Moore's home, studying and talking about issues in education. In addition, on those weekends that I didn't go home to the farm, you could find me at Sunday dinner with the Moore family. The impact that Mrs. Moore had on me when I was seven years old and the bond that we formed led me to a career in education and a desire to focus on relationship-building in my own classroom.

Now, as I have been teaching for over thirty years in the area of early childhood education, Mrs. Moore is on my mind each and every day. She was the first teacher, of so many, to have a positive impact on my life. I do my best to emulate the care and compassion I learned very early on from Mrs. Moore. The relationships teachers build with their students can be long-lasting. What I learned from Maxine Moore is that you never know how your influence on the life of a child will impact them! In all that you do, show every child that you love them and want what's best for them. Her care, compassion, and life-long connection started with a second-grader who needed her. She had no idea what the long-lasting and far-reaching impact would be. Yet she inspired a life of learning and a life of teaching. Her gentle guidance kept me headed in the right direction.

Each teacher after her added and guided in their own ways. The connections and the relationships built on each other. I hope and believe that their ripple continues to build into a current of positivity with my own students. That ripple reaches out in directions and guides in ways we may never even know. My life was forever changed by caring educators. The impact of that change continues.

Kris Jenkins received her bachelor's in elementary and early childhood education with a minor in music education, and a master's in education from Baker University. She has taught in Nebraska, California, Missouri, and Kansas, for over 33 years, all at the early childhood and kindergarten level. Her passion is learning more about being trauma-informed & trauma-responsive. She has been married for over 29 years to Chuck and has three grown children.

CHAPTER 8: RELATIONSHIPS

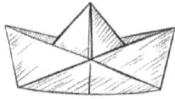

Discussing The Greatness Inside: The Good News Call Of The Day

by Chuck Moss

Five minutes can change your life and the lives of those around you. I had served as an assistant principal at the elementary and secondary levels for years, but then I was given the remarkable responsibility of leading Southside Elementary School in Dinwiddie County, Virginia. In my years in administration, I have become more and more convinced that relationships, on all fronts, must come before learning can occur. I have changed my focus to building relationships with staff, students, parents, the leadership team of my school division, and of our county, as a whole.

I pride myself on being able to find the common thread with individuals throughout a diverse population. I have always been able to find the one thing about which a frustrated parent, teacher, or child wants to talk and that allows me to get past the hurdles of distrust that educators, especially administrators, so often face. Over my two decades in education I have found that starting off a conversation on a topic of common interests helps to ease tension and helps to build a bond. It helps form trust in the relationship.

I have had conversations about everything from selecting the right fishing lure to co-parenting. I've started conversations about comic books, leadership, movies, cars, interior design, and the always popular topic, the weather. At some point, the person at the other end of the conversation has to decide to trust me enough to share their story about what is truly frustrating them. That trust is how we, as human beings, begin to build our relationships. And it can lead to some really helpful progress.

One of the main challenges I faced as a new elementary principal was coming into a school with the highest English Language Learner (ELL) population in our county. I quickly came to recognize that our

Spanish-speaking families had an inherent distrust in our system because they assumed that my role as an administrator is also to serve as an adjunct arm of the Immigration and Customs Enforcement service. That, of course, is not my role; instead my role is to make sure that learning and our curriculum are accessible to all students, regardless of their backgrounds. Convincing some ELL families of that has been a difficult task, even with the help of a dedicated ELL teacher. I realized something, however, that allowed me to form an instant connection with our families, no matter the language they spoke at home. Inspiration came to me from another educator I connected with through Twitter.

Dr. Mark French is an elementary school principal in Minnesota. I was looking at his Twitter feed (@PrincipalFrench) when I took notice of something he created called, "Good News Call of the Day" (#GoodNewsCalloftheDay). Dr. French takes five minutes each day to call home about a student's positive impact at school. I'm grateful for the relationship that Twitter has allowed me to form with Dr. French, and how it can be credited with my discovery and use of the "Good News Call of the Day." The connection I formed with him, and his influence on me, have allowed me to form so many more meaningful relationships this year.

I quickly realized that this positive call home was one that had devotees from around the globe. It is an accepted truth that positive contact with families builds an educator's credibility with families, but rarely have I seen it done with such fidelity as with Mark's, "Good News Call of the Day." I was impressed and decided I would try it. The first few times I called home the impact on the family members I called was immediate, and I realized that I had stumbled onto something that was going to be a useful tool in my toolbox. Little did I know how useful a tool it would become.

The "Good News Call of the Day" has developed a momentum of its own and has become one of my most powerful tools because it helps build relationships with families and those relationships lead to trust. Everyone in our building is focusing on being positive, trying to shine the light on others that are making positive contributions to our school culture. Everyone has become involved: students stop me in the hall or the cafeteria to tell my why they deserve the "Good News Call of the Day," teachers make suggestions about who deserves a call, our office staff makes suggestions, and every person with any ownership in our school has come to appreciate the "Good News Call of the Day."

My favorite example of how the "Good News Call of the Day" specifically helped build relationships with the ELL population at Southside Elementary was the first time I made the call to a Spanish-speaking parent. With my ELL teacher there to translate for me, I could hear the change in the parent's voice as the news was shared that their child was our MVP that day. The quiet, guarded tone with which the conversation began was soon replaced by an enthusiastic voice bursting with pride at the thought that her child was being recognized at our school for greatness rather than a shortcoming. I had hoped that our conversation would have a positive impact on our MVP student and her family. The next day, I found out just how impactful the conversation was.

One of my favorite parts of the day is my time each morning welcoming students and parents to our school. The morning after I made the call home with the help of our ELL teacher, I found my handshake being pumped vigorously by a young lady. I had seen and welcomed her to our building on many mornings, though she had never responded to my greetings before. She was obviously the mother of yesterday's MVP student. Then, the young lady herself even greeted me. Although my ELL teacher wasn't available to translate, this mom knew enough English when paired with my middling Spanish, that we were able to communicate enough for me to confirm she was the parent with whom I had spoken the previous day. She smiled, hugged me, and as she walked back to her car, turned and waved at least a half-dozen more times.

What was different? I had greeted her almost daily from the dog days of September through the turning of the leaves in October. She had never responded before, but today she was the one who initiated contact. What was different today that made both mom and daughter interact with me? What was different was that caring educators in our building alerted me to the amazing work this young woman was accomplishing. I took five minutes to connect with her and her family and focused on the relationship. We built trust and created relationships where none had existed. The relationships were the difference.

Because of the five minute phone call, we now had something in common—we both believed in the greatness inside her child and because of the "Good News Call of the Day," now we both knew it. The power of relationships cannot be overstated and the power of the "Good News Call of the Day" in building those relationships makes it one of the most useful tools in my educational toolbox.

You can accomplish so much in five minutes a day. Five minutes can change your life and the lives of those around you. You can change the entire culture of your building and maybe the whole community by focusing on relationships.

Chuck Moss *has served in education for more than two decades. As a teacher, coach, and principal, he has been dedicated to building relationships with, and learning the stories of, the people in the community which he serves. He believes that relationships are the key to creating partnerships with students and families and that those partnerships are, in turn, the key to success.*

CHAPTER 9: RELATIONSHIPS

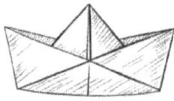

We Need You. It's An Emergency.
by Brian Kulak

The familiar creaky-door-opening sound followed by the inviting ringing alert stopped me in my tracks. Before text messaging, AOL Instant Messenger was as close as we came to on-demand communication, and I left my account on and open all the time. I was going to let it go. Check it later. I had just grabbed a beer and was heading to my living room to watch the Flyers. It was a Thursday night in mid-spring, and I was beat after a long day of teaching and coaching baseball. But I doubled back to my office to find what seemed like an urgent message in neon blue.

Beccalyne413: Kulak are you there? We need you. It's an emergency.

For each of the fifteen years I was a high school English and journalism teacher, I introduced my students, and later their parents, to English IV by insisting that everything we would do together would be built on a foundation of making connections. We would make connections to the text. With the language. With our writing. And, most importantly, with each other. If we didn't make connections, I assured them, then I wasn't doing my job.

The school in which I taught was a tiny 7th-12th grade building in southern New Jersey. Like many fortunate teachers, I returned to teach at my alma mater, in 1999, just five years after I graduated. So not only were there familiar student faces, my brother's among them, but there were also familiar faculty faces. For most of them, I was as uncomfortable dropping their formal titles as I was accepting my own. Still, I was home. I was where I was supposed to be.

When I took the job, I was told that I would be teaching a full load, six classes, four of which were classes of seniors because, as my supervisor told me, "no one else wanted them." Though a curious decision at the time, I was only 22, living at home, and my brother was on my roster, I accepted it with genuine enthusiasm. This was a group, I decided, that would help define what kind of teacher I would be.

As it turned out, the teacher I would be was a little different than other members of my department. I loathed lecturing and assigning compliance-based worksheets and activities, so I just sort of stopped. Rather, I asked the kids how they wanted to learn, allowed them to form their own groups and provide each other feedback, and started a weekly public speaking activity called The Hot Seat. The result was the genesis of that annual promise to my kids that we would make connections.

Without human connections, I thought, what am I even doing? Little did I know that the connections I had built with my students were deeper and more meaningful than I ever imagined. The connections we had made would save a life.

Beccalyne413: Kulak are you there? We need you. It's an emergency.
Brikool11: Who is this?
Beccalyne413: It's Becca. Karly is here, too. It's Greg. He's in real bad shape. I think he might do something to himself.
Brikool11: Whoa, whoa, whoa. Slow down. What happened?
Beccalyne413: He's talking crazy. He's crying. Sara was cheating on him. They broke up. He wants to kill himself. Idk.
Brikool11: Alright, can you get him to the school? Can we meet in my room?
Beccalyne413: We'll try. C u soon.

I began to process the intensity of the conversation that just took place. Of the many things that didn't occur to me in that moment: how did these two students get my screenname? Of all the ways to approach someone in crisis, why this way? Why me? Should I call someone? Was it a bad idea to meet them after 9pm in my classroom on a Thursday night?

With time to gather my thoughts, I decided to call the proper authorities and let them know the situation. I let them know that students were going to meet me in my classroom and that one seemed suicidal.

Immediately after the call, I drove to my school, opened up my room, turned on the lights and waited. And waited. And waited. You know that feeling when you're waiting for someone to emerge from surgery, and you know the person will be the same but they may look totally different? It may take that person a second to register what just happened to them? This was exactly like that but rather than emerging from something, we were about to enter into it.

When I heard them shuffling up the steps toward my room, I was all at once relieved because they got him there *and* terrified of what he might look like. With his hat pulled down over his eyes, a beat up hoodie with sweatpants, and slides, he looked like he always did. This was Greg: a student I'd known for years, a talented member of our baseball team and a goofball who reveled in his own relative cluelessness. But when he lifted his head to meet my gaze, he wasn't Greg. He was a red-faced, swollen-eyed shell of the kid who was always smiling in most other situations. In fact, it was hard at that point to picture what his smile even looked like.

As we waited for professionals to arrive, my three students explained the pain Greg was feeling. Greg's girlfriend, Sara, who was also a student of mine, treated Greg about as poorly as a person can. She manipulated him, she emasculated him, she cheated on him, she made fun of him. And he took it all. Until tonight.

"Dude, are you thinking of killing yourself?" I asked.
"I dunno. I guess. What's the point?" he said.
"You want to kill yourself because of Sara?" I asked.
"I mean I dunno. I hate her. I can't believe this is happening," he said.

With exactly zero counseling training, I trusted my instincts and wanted to keep Greg with me where I knew he was safe. I was able to keep him talking for just about the entire time he was there. The girls chimed in when they felt they could help, and slowly he started to admit how much he had to live for. Then, because I needed him to know that from this point on we would be forever connected, I shared the story of my own devastating breakup from my college girlfriend, whom I was convinced I would marry. Though the circumstances were different, I wanted him to see me as someone he could relate to, as someone who had lived through the pain he was feeling and who came out on the other side.

By the end of our conversation, the four of us cried together, shared a group hug straight out of an episode of *Saved by the Bell*, and promised to continue to always check in with each other. I'll never know why they chose me to help Greg that night because I never asked, and it didn't seem to matter. Somehow, they connected with each other through our time in my class. We built trust and a solid relationship in our class so they connected me to Greg, and on that night, we connected Greg with his life.

Greg continued to find the importance of his life and took advantage of the experiences he would've otherwise missed out on.

Some twelve years after that transcendent experience, I was still connected to Greg. I had an extra ticket to the last Pearl Jam concert in Philadelphia. I posted the free ticket on Facebook, and it was Greg who first contacted me and scooped it up. It was his first Pearl Jam show, and it was great to see him next to me, enjoying life, in awe as he watched the concert. I can't promise he didn't notice, but there were several times during the show when I peeked over at him, just to make sure he was really there.

Recently, my adult baseball team needed a shortstop. I reached out to Greg, an outstanding high school player, and asked if he wanted to play. He answered immediately, "Of course!"

On opening day, after I delivered a mediocre fastball to the leadoff hitter, it was Greg who fielded the grounder, tripped near the mound, and rolled over right next to me. It was the first time we had played together. When he handed me the ball, I just said, "Dude." He replied, "I have no idea," smiled, and went back to his place at shortstop.

These moments remind me how important our jobs are as educators. The value and time I put into relationship-building helped save Greg's life. Although I don't share data here to prove how the relationships we have built in our classroom have had a positive impact on the lives of students, we do have Greg's life to prove it mattered. We'll all get tripped up from time to time, but it's important we continue to foster relationships that matter so we can be there for those who need us.

Brian Kulak is a K-5 building administrator in New Jersey. Before that, he taught high school English and journalism for fifteen years. Brian is the founder of leveluplead.com, a teaching, learning, and leadership blog, and author of an upcoming book of the same name. He has written for Edutopia and Educational Viewpoints. He has spoken at the NCTE/CEL conference, at ECET2NJPA, and at various Edcamps in New Jersey. He is a devoted family man, a baseball fanatic, and a Pearl Jam aficionado.

CHAPTER 10: RELATIONSHIPS

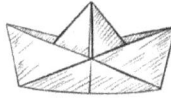

Secret Handshakes and High Fives
by Kailee Drewno

Building relationships is hands-down the most important aspect of teaching. As a first-year teacher and having the so-called "rough group" of sixth graders, building relationships became the focus of my year. My school year started out with teachers and other community members telling me how difficult my class was going to be. Everywhere I turned someone had something negative to say. Staying positive and proving them wrong was my number one goal and the eventual highlight of my year.

My students are some of the brightest, kindest, loving individuals out there. Of course, they sometimes exhibit behaviors that are not good, but as a teacher, part of our job is to teach our students right from wrong. There are so many reasons as to why our students behave a certain way. If I could take all of my students troubles away, I would in a heartbeat. The majority of my students live in a low socioeconomic area, receive free and reduced lunch, and come from broken families or are in foster care. Despite any obstacles they faced at home, it did not take me long to realize that the only thing my students really needed was a loving adult that refused to give up on them, believe in them, and teach them how to believe in themselves.

I started building relationships with my students before the school year started. I met almost all of my students the day before school officially started at our school's annual meet-and-greet. I made sure to learn all of my students' names, find out about what they did on their summer vacation, and find common interests that we might share. When they came to school the next day they were stunned that I was able to remember all of their names and some of their interests. When it comes to building relationships, teachers have to make an effort to get to know every little thing about their students. We need to know what they like to be called, what they are interested in, whether they have siblings or pets, what makes them happy, angry, or sad, their goals, and their strengths and weaknesses. Not only did I learn about them and continue to learn about them, but I also let them learn about me. I shared my likes, dislikes, and the experiences I had that have helped shape me into the person I am today. My students even looked me up on the internet because they wanted to know more about me. At first I was a little taken aback by that, but my principal said, "That just means they like you." I continued to find ways to build on the relationship.

As the year went on, I made a conscious effort to greet my students at the door every morning and do a secret handshake or a high five with each and every one of them. This let the students know that I was excited to see them and was eager to know how their weekend or night had been. Also, I made a conscious effort to really listen to them. Whenever my students had something to share, I tried to give them my undivided attention. This was an important thing to do because I might have been the only person listening. The more I opened up to them the more they opened up to me and to each other. I found out these were not the students I was warned to be afraid of. I learned that my students are some of the brightest, kindest, most loving individuals. I looked for more ways to get to know my students.

While many teachers enjoy the break from students by eating in the staff dining area, I offered my students the opportunity to eat lunch with me and others in our classroom. This gave the students an opportunity to share whatever they wanted with me. One day during lunch I told the students about how I loved to dance. A few of the girls asked me if we could create a dance and perform it at the upcoming school dance, and I agreed. We practiced during lunch for a few days and then performed it at the dance. They were nervous to actually dance in front of their friends, but I kept telling them that they would be awesome. Because we shared this common interest and took the risk together, it inspired one of the girls who loved doing the dance so much that she now attends dance classes.

One of the simplest and most powerful ways I built relationships was by writing my students notes every so often telling them what I thought they needed to hear. During the week of Thanksgiving, I wrote my students notes expressing why I was thankful to have them in my class. On one student's note I wrote that Aaron should believe in himself because I believe in him, and I know that he will accomplish great things. Aaron started off the year sad and hating himself. Every day I would tell him that I was glad he came to school. Every time he had negative self-talk saying that he could not do something, I would tell him that he could do anything he set his mind to especially if he kept on trying. Then one day something clicked for Aaron. He started to come to school with a smile on his face. He came up to me and said, "Thank you for believing in me. Because of you, I now believe in myself." I found more ways to send simple yet powerful notes throughout the year when my students needed them most.

State testing can be a stressful time for students. I wrote notes to each of my students before state testing to tell them how proud I was of them and that they should not stress about the test because it is just a test. I told them that what mattered to me was that they tried their absolute best. I am convinced my students know that I will be there for them through thick and thin. While writing notes became a powerful tool, I wanted to do more.

Supporting my students meant not only knowing about their activities, but also being there to watch them participate in their activities. Many of my students did not have enough adults in their life cheering them on. I knew I could help boost their confidence and passion for their activities by simply being there. I helped foster meaningful relationships by supporting my students in the activities that they did outside of school. I attended quite a few different sporting events. After each event I made sure to find my students and tell them that I was impressed by their effort.

One of my students, Kyle, who had a hard time opening up to me throughout the year, asked me to go to his wrestling tournament. Kyle often had difficulties doing his work and was often in trouble for distracting others. His wrestling match was an hour and a half away from where I lived, but I decided that I needed to go. I wanted him to know that I cared and would support him in this activity that he loved and was exceptionally good at. I don't think he expected me to go because when I got there, he came over all excited and happy to see me. Between matches he continued to come over to me with the biggest smile on his face and talked to me about what was going on. After that wrestling tournament Kyle began doing his work and stopped getting in trouble in my class. Although I was not his main teacher, when he had free time he would stop by my classroom to talk with me. I was also honored when he asked to eat lunch in my room. The few hours I spent that day driving and watching Kyle's wrestling match completely changed our relationship and proved to him that someone cared.

There would be more opportunities to be involved in my students' lives outside of school. James was a boy who had a lot of energy, was always willing to help his classmates, but who tended to get in trouble when asked to do something he did not want to do. One day James asked me to attend his basketball game. It was close to where I live, so I decided to attend. The game was on a Saturday and James was very concerned that I would not be there because the time of the game had changed. He kept asking his mother to email me to make sure that I was given the correct time and address. His mother did, and she added that James was so excited that I was coming and that he could not stop talking about it. It melted my heart that this boy wanted me to be at his game. Because of the time I devoted to building relationships in the classroom, he knew that I played basketball when I was younger. Now, he wanted to show me what he had learned about the game so far. Attending that basketball game for James made all the difference in his behavior and attitude for the rest of the school year.

Building relationships might take effort, but I know that the effort is worth the outcomes. My students know that they have someone who will be cheering them on for life. My students know that I think they are some of the brightest, kindest, most loving individuals out there. I want my students to know that if they ever need anything, they can always reach out and I'll be there.

Looking back at the teachers I had growing up, my favorites were the ones who cared and took the time to build a relationship with me. These teachers are still in my life today; supporting me, giving me advice, and believing in me. I've learned that you will probably not build relationships with each of your students all at once. Sometimes it takes longer with certain students than it does with others. You have to stay positive and find that one thing that will help you make a connection. Building relationships will help students trust you and want to learn. Students will be able to express themselves freely and feel safe. You can be the reason why they chose to never give up. You can be the reason why they are confident. You can be the reason why they pursue something they are passionate about. Do not think for a second that you do not make an impact. Because you do. Every single day.

Kailee Drewno *is a sixth grade science and ELA teacher in upstate New York. She is passionate about science, technology, makerspace, and robotics. Some of her goals are to help her students believe in themselves and help them find enjoyment in what they are learning. She learned as a first year teacher that building relationships with students can create a positive culture and can make students want to learn and come to school every day.*

CHAPTER 11: RELATIONSHIPS

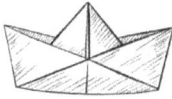

The Midnight Hour is Close at Hand
by Jon Spike

When I was about seven years old, my classmates and I decided we were going to catch a leprechaun.

We hatched the plan in the waning moments before the last recess of the day. We approached our second-grade teacher, Ms. Nelson, and asked what she thought of our scheme.

"Why not? Go chase that leprechaun," she told us.

Through some combination of luck and foolish optimism, we searched the expansive playground high and low for any signs of a leprechaun and, incredibly, a clue emerged. Nestled in some tall grass near the creek that ran around our elementary school, we found a mangled piece of plastic that just so happened to resemble the vest of a leprechaun. We eagerly rushed back to the classroom with our dirty, disfigured treasure.

"Look Ms. Nelson! We found a leprechaun vest!"

At the time, we did not realize the gravity of the decision Ms. Nelson faced. She looked at the mud-covered plastic and declared, "You sure did. Let's talk about it in class." For the next few minutes, the class gathered around and heard us retell the story of how we nearly found a leprechaun, settling for his vest instead.

I cannot tell you much of what I learned in the second grade. I vaguely remember a unit on Australia. I think we made ice cream one day with a bucket and lots of stirring. I can, however, recite nearly every detail about chasing that leprechaun.

Nearly 17 years later, I entered my third year as a high school English teacher in suburban Wisconsin. I had the opportunity to be a facilitator for our new Freshman Seminar program, a course to help first-year students learn the ins and outs of high school in a safe and connected community. That first iteration, to put it bluntly, was a failure. My students rarely felt compelled to discuss pertinent issues, collaborate on meaningful projects, or really interact with each other much outside of the classroom walls. All of the goals we had for the program seemed unrealized, and I put the blame squarely on myself for not fostering a better sense of community.

I vowed to make this year different. The only problem was that I had no new ideas about how to make any meaningful change happen.

Thankfully, a spark of inspiration came in the form of a challenge from our Technology Director, Diane. She sent out a district-wide email about a contest from an educational technology company. The premise was simple: create a parody music video about why you need new technology in the classroom.

This was *it*! I thought maybe—just maybe—if we had a challenge that required teamwork, creativity, and everyone contributing their talents, we could naturally come together as a learning community.

The first goal, of course, was to spark student interest. I realized that the students would not buy in if it feels forced. I hatched a plan to introduce the contest without seeming like we *had* to do it.

During one of our sessions, I gave the students some work time, and I casually walked over to my computer. Feigning surprise, I stopped them all for an announcement.

"I just got the strangest email today. Something about a contest," I said, beginning to read the pertinent details. "Looks like they're looking for classes to make a … a parody music video. Hey, first prize earns new technology swag!"

Heads lifted out of books and smartphone screens. Whispers emerged at tables.

I continued. "I dunno. What do you think?"

Voices piped up from the crowd of first-year high schoolers.

"I think it would be fun."

"What if we did 'Gangnam Style'? That would be hilarious."

Jon Spike

"Why not?"

The seed was planted. Now all I had to do was figure out how to make a music video.

The next class, we jumped in head-first with a brainstorming session. We decided that we needed a song to parody before anything could happen with a storyline, strategy, or otherwise.

We heard everything from "Gangnam Style" to "Call Me Maybe" to "Don't Stop Believin'." Then, lightning struck.

"What about 'Thriller' by Michael Jackson?" offered a sheepish voice in the back. Aside from two or three students who made me feel ancient by asking who Michael Jackson was, the students loved the idea. And who could blame them? It was a perfect mix of classic and well-known. The song already had a plot, so all we had to do was remix it to fit the need for the technology requirement for the contest.

One of my favorite teacher movies of all time is "School of Rock," and I never thought I would see the day where my classroom turned into a recreation of the film. Sure enough, students began volunteering for their roles. We had songwriters working on remixing the lyrics to create a story. Others were planning shots based on the premise of the lyrics. At one point, we discussed ways we could film a hand emerging from the ground without actually having to bury someone underground. A few brave souls signed up to be vocalist, and we had a handful of students offer their services to help sing the chorus.

A few classes into the project, I felt a tug on my shirt. One of the quietest students in my class looked up at me and said, "Mr. Spike, we want to choreograph a dance for the music video."

"That's great! But there's already a 'Thriller' dance."

"I know, but we want to make something better."

That's all I needed to hear. With the green light, she dashed off to a group of friends to begin planning their dance routine.

The true beauty of the project came during workshop time in our sessions. I would remind myself to stop and look out at the interactions happening in the room: a huddle of students practicing the chorus together, another group creating technology props for the beginning montage, and other students scouting locations to shoot the scenes from the script. Laughter emerged constantly from a flubbed line or a ridiculous-looking item created by our prop team. Conversations carried outside of our short class time and into the hallways. Community blossomed out of our little three-minute production.

We finally reached our time to film, and the brilliant part was that our script allowed for anyone to be in the film who wanted a role. Those who did not want to be in it ran cameras, placed props, and gave notes on each take's effectiveness. Many of our locations required filming after school, and the attendance for these shoots was incredible. Students owned this project, and they wanted to see their baby come to fruition in the best possible way.

After months of brainstorming, writing, filming, and editing, our creation was finished and submitted. It had everything: students coming back from the dead, old typewriters, and one amazing scene where the zombie students literally rip off one of my arms (don't worry, I get the arm back and use it to "cure" them of their zombie conditions). We even manage to work in the famous "Scooby Doo" chase sequence, where the students pursue me into one door of a hallway, and I somehow emerge from another door seconds later.

With our creation complete, we had plenty of time to watch the other entrants' creations online and see what others had submitted to the contest. Instead of jealousy and resentment, the students showed genuine interest in how each group approached the challenge. We saw entire schools do a massive, choreographed dance and a green-screen voyage to the moon.

By the time our project was done, I did not have to worry about building community the rest of the school year. Once the students connected through a common goal, they were friends both inside and outside of our classroom walls.

Seventeen years prior, my teacher let us chase the leprechaun. She let us do something ridiculous and then let us share our experience with others. When I thought about why we did the parody music video contest, I could not help but think it was our chance to chase the leprechaun.

Walt Whitman wrote, "The powerful play goes on, and you may contribute a verse." The most important goal we should have as educators is to help students find the verse they will contribute to the world. If we give them a chance to chase the leprechaun, our students will have no trouble discovering what their verse will be.

Jon Spike *is the Coordinator of Instructional Technology & Integration Services at University of Wisconsin-Whitewater where he teaches courses such as Video Games & Learning and Digital Tools. He previously worked as a high school English teacher and a technology integrator before entering his current role. Jon is passionate about helping students share their work with a global audience, implementing game-based learning, and integrating technology into the classroom. Check out his website at www.jonspike.com.*

CHAPTER 12: HOOKS

A *Salon* With A View
by Jason Bretzmann

When I did my student teaching, I watched another student teacher teach European history by having students immerse themselves in the people of the time and act out what she called a *salon*. She explained that in the 1700s the best and the brightest scientists, mathematicians, poets, and thinkers of the time got together in a room and discussed the issues of the day. It was the Age of Reason. It was the Enlightenment.

In my U.S. history classes that semester (and for about ten years after it), I started by explaining that the ideas of the Enlightenment helped lead to the American republic. And those ideas were developed by the best and the brightest scientists, mathematicians, poets, leaders, and thinkers of their time. I continued to tell my students that in the spirit of that tradition, I asked our school administration to put the best and the brightest that our school had to offer in my classes. Then I'd use both hands, palms open, to present them to each other: "Ladies and Gentlemen, I give you the best and the brightest that Muskego High School has to offer." They'd chuckle and sometimes roll their eyes, but were mostly willing to play along.

"And as such, we have to opportunity and the responsibility…nay… *the duty* to engage in deep conversations to discuss the issues of the day."

I'd tell my students that this coming Friday, we would engage in our first *salon*. By Wednesday they should each bring a question that had at least two sides to the answers. I gave students a slip of paper to write their questions on and told them we would put them in a hat and that the first person to talk would get to choose the next question from the hat. We would, indeed, discuss the issues of the day: according to the best and the brightest that our school had to offer. The questions and the answers would come from them.

They showed up with great questions. Some were silly or small: *What's your favorite color and why?* or *Does candy cost too much?* Some were deep and unusual: *How much does happiness weigh?* or *When will the world end and how do you know?* Some were simple yet important: *What do you want to be when you grow up and why?* or *Do you support the death penalty, or not?* We answered them all.

But I always started with the following question to get our classes talking. You are in charge of 100 people who are in danger. You have two options to save them. The first option would surely work, but it would save 90 of the 100 people. The other option would save all 100 people, but has a 50 percent chance of working. Which option would you choose and why?

After a few years, I noticed that it was a predictable sequence of events for each group. One student would ask what kind of danger it was (deserted island, lava, fire, etc.). A few would try to negotiate and finagle another ten people into the rescue boat they created in their minds. And someone would ask if they were included in the 100 or not. My answer usually included another question, "How would your answer be different if you were or you weren't?"

Then the answers would start—also predictable over time. A few students would jump in and say that they would pick the 100 people because you have to try to save everybody. Someone would reply that it was too risky and that it was a 50/50 chance that everybody would die. Then someone would ask again if they were included in the group or not. Once in a while someone would blurt out that they would just let everyone fend for themselves and get the heck out of their on their own. (Self-preservation is an important thing for a high school sophomore.) But the deeper reflection would begin.

If you tried to save everybody and were successful, not only would you save a hundred people, you would also be a hero. Even if you tried and you weren't successful, you'd still be a hero just for trying (especially if you weren't included in the 100 and you perished trying to do heroic work).

Yes, they said, but what if you weren't successful and you got everybody killed? Isn't it better to save 90 of the people and have it be a sure thing? Wouldn't those 90 families be grateful that you got them home safety?

Yes, they said, but wait a minute. How would you choose the 10 who didn't get saved? Well, you could just ask for volunteers. Or you could just choose the oldest people because they've already lived a life so they should give the younger people a chance to have live a life too.

That's when it would get really interesting. I'd ask questions about whether some lives were more valuable. I'd ask the reasoning behind students' comments on this question. What makes a younger life more meaningful? Are old people "worthless?" Are older people "almost dead anyway" like he just suggested? I'd talk about how Grandma Moses started painting when she was in her late seventies and she became a famous painter. She contributed when she was older, right? Then, for those groups that could handle it, I'd go one step further. What if the older person were Grandma Moses or Ronald Reagan, or Mother Theresa and they were part of the 10? And what if you kept a young Saddam Hussein, Benito Mussolini, or Adolf Hitler alive because of their age? Does that change anyone's thinking or not?

What interesting, deep, expansive conversations we had. Students were hooked. They fully realized that nobody was really in danger, but they answered like the world, their world, depended on it. Sometimes it got heated. It was always interesting. Even when it wasn't, we just moved onto a new question and then it was interesting again. These were their questions and their answers and everybody had to listen. Everybody had to hear what they said, and everybody had a chance to say it. I kept a speaker's list and called on them in the order that they raised a hand. They were figuring out their place in the world and that there were others who thought like them. And others who really, *really* didn't. But mostly it was an opportunity to say something in school and be heard. By your classmates. By your teacher. They had something to say and this was their opportunity to say it. They felt like they were making a difference, and they loved it.

I got repeated requests to have a salon every Friday. Indeed, some students thought we did have a salon every Friday. I heard about that from at least one other teacher who ask how I could get through all the content when we just sat around and talked every Friday. I assured her that this was not the case, and that we learn the content quite nicely because my students are super-engaged. They are willing to share answers and thoughts on the content, and our comfort with each other helps to keep the class moving. No, the salon doesn't happen every Friday, but it could. In fact, in just one class it did.

We had just studied industrialization, robber barons, and organized labor in our U.S. history class. At the same time, students were really loving the opportunities to discuss in our salons (and that they didn't have to do "real work" on those days). The content and the salon join forces when a student named Clayton decided to unionize his class.

They held a vote. They elected Clayton president of the union. They wrote their demands. They voted on their demands. They instructed Clayton to present their demands to me.

I seized on the teachable moment and talked about labor and management and reasonable demands and offers and counter offers and job actions and protest and civil disobedience and more. As far as I could stretch this, I was going to keep it going. They were hooked.

I explained how in our current scenario that since they were labor, I was management. And as management, I was denying their requests to have salons every Friday. We had too much content to cover and not everybody fully participates anyway. It was not doable. It was not going to happen.

They persisted. They explained that if their demands were not met that they would engage in job actions. They were considering a work slowdown, or even going on strike. Some students cheered spontaneously and loudly for the strike. As that class period was ending, I told them that they would hear more of my response to the potential strike tomorrow. Let's keep this lesson going, I thought. Let's expand the teachable moment. Let's keep playing along.

As they left class, I headed from our room to the study hall nearby. Several students that I had in other classes and in previous years slowly meandered out of their study hall and I approached them. I told them the situation with Clayton, my students, and the impending strike. I asked them to consider crossing the potential picket line and coming to my class to do school work during that class hour instead of going to their study hall. They were immediately all-in. I had lined up scab workers to take the place of my actual students!

The next day I informed the class that management would not accept their demands and that if they went on strike I had replacement workers lined up to take their place. No big deal for me. I've been to study hall, I told them, and they looked like better workers anyway. And they'd be less trouble too. They gasped, murmured, and quickly consulted with each other. I smiled to myself and momentarily considered that not only were these students totally engaged, but the day before I had a small group of students in study hall spontaneously learning about labor, management, and U.S. history. We were taking the content beyond the walls of our classroom.

After a quick caucus between themselves, my students asked that since I was management, didn't I teach them that management should present a counter offer if they didn't like what labor was offering. I smiled again. They instructed me to present a counter offer. I couldn't disagree (or let on that I was impressed with their knowledge of labor relations), so I developed my counteroffer. I presented it to them in writing.

I made it so that they couldn't accept it. I wrote that each student would have to contribute each week in a meaningful way to the conversation in the salon. Each student would have to bring a new and substantive question each week. And each student would have to do all of the homework assignments from the textbook when I assigned them. I waited for their counter offer. It didn't come.

They discussed then voted. They voted to accept my terms and by so doing, accepted the idea that they would police themselves. They were going to make sure everyone complied because they knew that if someone didn't, the weekly *salon* would end. Some weeks it took more effort and some weeks it took cajoling. But most weeks everyone knew the expectations and they met them or exceeded them. Some students came with extra questions each week in case somebody didn't write theirs. Students encouraged each other to talk during the salon and that helped build onto a positive culture in the class. And students asked each other if they did their homework.

They would remind each other of the deadline and make sure everybody got it done.

The rest of that semester, we had a salon every week. We learned the content, too. Maybe more quickly. Maybe more deeply. Because now it had an added bonus that came along with it. Not to mention, we were part of it and we could see how history happens. We lived it. We negotiated and avoided a strike. We compromised, like Americans do, and we each got some of what we wanted and needed. It was real. And we were hooked because they were *our* ideas. And those ideas were developed by the best and the brightest scientists, mathematicians, poets, leaders, and thinkers of their time.

CHAPTER 13: HOOKS

You Had Me At Hello
by Kenny Bosch

"It's about to get awkward." "I hope you are okay with touching people?" "Did you line up a date for homecoming?" These are the first words students hear from me as they enter my room on the second day of school. You can see the worried and confused looks on their faces as they enter the classroom. They are unsure about what is going to happen next, and that is how I hook them into the lesson. When they enter the room, the hook is firmly set.

The song, "Getting to Know You," by James Taylor is playing in the background and on the whiteboard in red letters are the words, "Speed Dating." The desks are lined up in groups of two facing each other. If I could, I would have real candles burning and mood lighting, but I think I've probably pushed the students far enough. After all, it is only the second day of school and open flames are against fire code!

Over the past ten years I've seen a real shift in my students, and not for the better, when it comes to what many call soft skills. I find that with each passing year they are more comfortable being alone and looking into one of their many screens and avoiding the real world. I wanted to find a way to jump start my students' willingness to speak in class with an activity that would push them past the fear of talking to new people. I wanted to do this in a fun, unique way.

We have all been in classes or groups where you are supposed to stand up, state your name, and share something interesting about yourself. I hate these ice-breakers. They are predictable and don't allow for real communication. I have found myself wanting to answer with, "Hello, my name is Kenny Bosch. Something interesting about me is that I hate ice-breakers," and then sit down. I don't hate ice-breakers due to fear of public speaking, or not knowing what to say. I hate them because they are boring and unnatural. It seems that many people spend the time of an ice-breaker thinking about themselves and some "interesting fact" instead of listening to everyone else in the room. By the end of the activity, all you remember is that you don't remember much about anyone else and that you need a better interesting fact for the next time an ice-breaker activity happens. I wanted something more. Something better. I wanted to have my students really get to know each other in a meaningful way, and I was looking for a method to help them feel confident enough to talk to new students.

Once the students are in the room and seated, I turn off the music and explain to them that we are not actually going to be speed dating, but rather participating in a speed get-to-know-you activity. To begin, I tell the students that we are going to be together for about an hour a day for 180 days. We will get to see each other more than most of our family members and we should get to know each other. Once I had settled their minds a little bit, it was time to hook them again.

The second hook I used was a student guinea pig. I look around the room for the face of a student that I know and ask them to shake my hand, as if we are meeting each other for the first time. I ask the class to pick one of us to study closely during the handshake. After the handshake I ask them what they noticed? For a moment, I feel bad for the selected student because he or she has to shake my hand about ten times as I demonstrate all of the incorrect ways to shake hands. "In our country," I like to say, "we don't do it like this..." Then I get to have some fun as I act out for the students poor body language, poor eye contact, and the real crowd pleasers that get the students laughing. I demonstrate the "dead fish hand" handshake and the most egregious handshake of them all, the triangle/half handshake! Students laugh as I form my fingers into a little triangle and allow that weird group of finger tips to be "shook."

Students are yelling out, "Who shakes hands like that?" Other students answer back, "My mom does!" Invariably, at least one student will say in a moment of self-realization, "I shake hands like that." Instead of standing in front of the room and giving a "lesson" on proper etiquette and handshakes, I hook them with funny examples and empower them to be more confident as they are about to participate in the speed getting-to-know-you activity.

The students are engaged, laughing, and learning all at the same time. It's a continuous hook that helps teach what I want students to know, but also communicates that we'll learn more than content in this class.

My next hook includes tricking another student into volunteering in front of the class by challenging their competitiveness. The night before this lesson, I asked each student to pick three questions from a list of 100 questions. They were to have those three questions ready for the next day and to make sure that the questions they chose would be ones that they would like to ask to someone else. I ask the group, "Who thinks they have the three best questions to ask someone?" I pick one of those students to help me demonstrate the next part of the lesson.

Without knowing it, the student will demonstrate the wrong way to ask questions to a person. They will ask me a question, "Do you have any pets?" I answer, "No." They ask me a second question, I give another one word answer, and we repeat this for the third question. The whole process takes about 10 seconds, it is awkward, and the room feels uneasy. I then ask the volunteer, "Can I try asking those same three questions?" The student agrees and I ask the same three questions and demonstrate how to be involved in a conversation by asking follow-up questions, listening to the answers, and being active in the conversation.

"Do you have any pets?" The student answers, "Yes." I ask how many? They respond, "Three pets." I ask "What are they, dogs or cats or...."" The student says, "Dogs." and I ask, "What are their names?" I continue to listen and ask follow-up questions for thirty seconds, and we never even get to the second question. Then I ask the students, "What makes a great conversation?" and they rattle off a bunch of great answers. We are now actually ready for our speed get-to-know-you activity.

By this time we had taken 10-15 minutes to set up the activity with a number of hooks and examples. Students are no longer scared and worried about going around the room and having speed-dating-style conversations, instead they are excited to get to know their classmates and are better prepared to meet new people. They have confidence in their introduction and have the tools to better participate in a conversation. The time and effort we put into a meaningful ice-breaking activity pays off for the entire school year.

Students continued to refer to my handshake examples and recalled how to be actively involved in a conversation. Sometimes they would point out, in a good-natured way, how a classmate was doing it incorrectly. Now *they* were setting the hooks. Because I hooked students in the beginning and continued to hook them, they had learned about doing things the right way. They learned about each other, and they were willing to continue that process for the rest of our time together. And who knows? While it wasn't my goal, maybe somebody did line up a date for homecoming.

Kenny Bosch *is an award-winning educator, author and project coordinator. During his 20-year career in education, he's been a leader in ed tech applications and instruction as both a classroom teacher and adjunct online professor. Kenny lives in Wisconsin and coaches numerous basketball teams.*

CHAPTER 14: HOOKS

Puppet Master
by Barbara Gruener

After fifteen years as a high school Spanish teacher and then a guidance counselor, I took a leap of faith and applied for a completely different job. I went to work with a Pre-K through 3rd grade school, mostly because I'd been encouraged by a friend to come to her sister school. But I also couldn't shake the feeling that the teens I was working with needed more social and emotional learning and skills practice at an earlier age. I was ready to respond to that feeling by securing this entirely new role at Westwood Elementary early that summer. I eagerly awaited meeting my new superheroes. As I was moving in, I was greeted by Seymour the seal, an adorable white baby harp seal puppet with his tags still on. Seems the counselor before me had purchased him but had not yet had a chance to get his feet wet, so to speak.

It is well-known that play is our ticket to engagement, but having come from a secondary background, I'd never really played with puppets before. Still, I figured he wasn't there waiting for me by chance. Seymour was there for a reason. This was a completely different job.

I gave Seymour a personality. He was shy so I wouldn't have to make him talk! I brought him to life on my hand. On the first day at my new school there we were, Seymour and me, standing at the door to greet our new friends. I was astounded at how the children at every age and stage (even their parents!) reacted to and connected with Seymour. He and I were inseparable; students pretty much thought of us as one and the same. If students saw me at school and I didn't have him with me, they would ask, "Where's Seymour?" or "How is Seymour today?" as if he were real. My first big mistake was on the day of the first fire drill when, in my rush to exit the building, I left Seymour behind. The kids were so nervous and worried about

Seymour. They do know that he's a puppet, right? I thought this to myself more than once. It really was a different job.

As the years went on, I found some friends for Seymour. There was Lucille the gray seal who had a pink bow in her hair, Henrietta the hen, Spike the porcupine, Junior the giraffe, and more. But the students from my first year mostly loved Seymour. Almost ten years later, when they were seniors in high school, I put Seymour on my hand for old time's sake and took him on a field trip to see those teenagers and say hello. It melted my heart to watch them reunite with their old buddy Seymour and share their memories about this little puffball of fur on my hand. One of them commented, "That little guy was my whole world."

When I was transferred to our sister school next door, my future with the puppets was a little uncertain. By third grade, some of the students had gotten too cool for my little puppet scenarios, so I thought my puppetry days were over. Not so, it would turn out. As soon as I got to the intermediate school, students greeted me with, "Did you bring the puppets? Did Seymour come, too?" I told them Seymour lived at Westwood Elementary and had to stay there. When I told them that the puppets who belonged to me made the move, they squealed with delight. As the school year started and I was shaking hands at the door of our first counseling class, a fifth-grade boy whispered, "We missed you and your puppets!"

I began thinking: *Were these jobs really that different after all?*

That year, one of our puppets, Pack the rat, set the scene for our trustworthiness lesson. His pack was heavy, so I "care-fronted" him about what was in it. As we checked it out, we found that it was filled with my character rocks. He'd been packing away things that didn't belong to him. So the students worked with him to take responsibility for it, fix it, and make better choices. After the lesson, two third grade students decided to help fix the bigger problem. After recess they brought a pile of rocks and cement pieces to my office. I wasn't in there at the time, so they put those treasures next to Pack on the stage with a note that read, "To Pack Rat and Mrs. Gruener." Be still my heart. These leaders had given up recess time to bring rocks to Pack so that he didn't have to steal any more. Talk about unleashing the power of the puppet. Social and emotional progress was being made.

We've even used the puppets to help us grow through discipline referrals. I'll never forget the time we were having so much trouble with a young man who'd been writing and saying ugly things. We asked him, instead, to write the next puppet script as he was sitting in the calm-down corner. He perked right up, wondering which puppet would be next. I gave him a choice and he picked Patch the pirate. He created the most eloquent script. He wrote creatively about a pirate puppet looking for a ship. The Leader-Ship. Or the Friend-Ship. Or the Citizen-Ship. So insightful and spot on.

The students got so disappointed whenever I didn't have a puppet with me as I greeted them at the door. This past January, I chose not to begin a new lesson with a puppet because we needed the entire block of time to make Valentines for our soldiers. They were a bit sad, but they understood that our puppets were hibernating for the winter. The promise that Rainbow the toucan would be ready for them when the calendar turned to February lifted their spirits and got them refocused on the main tasks at hand.

I recently mentioned that I'd be retiring from public school after 34 years of shaping hearts and minds for the future. You might predict my fifth graders' first question: "Will you be taking the puppets with you, or will you be donating them?" Then there was a barrage of requests: "I'll take Junior! I want Winthrup. Can I have Pack? Simon is mine!"

Clearly we're hooked on puppets. From Pre-K to high school seniors. And me, too! But why?

Maybe we all need the social-emotional stability of seeing our "friends" and knowing that they are there for us. Even if they are puppets. Maybe we all need to practice our social-emotional skills, and maybe a puppet is just the person to help us do it. Maybe these jobs aren't all that different.

We want to share our childhood fun and fantasy. As we get older we like to relive those simpler times. We want to see ourselves in others and share the common humanity in all of us. Even if they show up in the inhuman world of puppets.

These jobs weren't all that different. Whether very young students or on the verge of graduation, my students connected with the positive essence of our puppets and all they represented. They knew the puppets weren't real, but for moments in time, they suspended that knowledge and learned about and saw the best of what real people could be. They learned these important lessons and knew that these furry, inanimate objects embodied the best of who we are and who we can be as people. And hopefully they applied those lessons in their own lives. They saw who they wanted to be and stayed connected to those ideals. And so did I. These weren't different jobs at all. And we probably never really retire from them. They continue, always, for all of us—people *and* puppets.

A nationally recognized speaker, school counselor, and author, **Barbara Gruener** *thrives on positively influencing character change, passionately helping people create caring connections, and intentionally improving school climate and culture. Her innovative, inspirational ideas are sparked by 34 years in education growing alongside learners from every age and stage. Her book,* What's Under Your Cape? *is filled with engaging empowerment strategies to help stakeholders stretch and grow in their character building.*

CHAPTER 15: HOOKS

Pitzen's Rules

by Jason Bretzmann

Late one night recently, a close friend from elementary school tagged me in a Facebook conversation to ask about Four Square. Red rubber ball. Four squares. Recess.

She asked about the rules we used back at Cooper Elementary School over 35 years ago. Half a dozen elementary school chums chimed in with comments and acknowledgements of their memories of "Pitzen's Rules." Here we were, adults with kids, and we were discussing the rules that somebody else's kid made up on the playground decades before. The set of rules he made weren't an assignment, a worksheet, or even a project. But every day at recess we lived them. We experienced them. We remembered.

As teachers, isn't that what we want? Whether we help create them, or students create them for themselves, don't we want experiences for our students? Experiences that they remember forever.

I set as my standard the "social movement project" that my students did years ago when I taught Sociology. It was the high-water mark of projects over the last twenty-plus years as a teacher. It felt like more than a project. It was real, and it was authentic.

Students went through the blood, sweat, and tears of creating, researching, and presenting a movement that they wanted to see happen in their school or beyond it. They invited guest speakers, interviewed government officials, met with administrators, worked to build their movement, and so much more. And they felt the profound frustration that not everyone agreed with them when they presented their progress to the rest of the class. It was real.

Some groups caused real change to happen. They made a bigger parking lot happen. They moved the mirrors that reflected, through an open bathroom door, boys using the urinal. And over a decade later, they finally realized a doubling of passing time between semester exams. Whether they caused change or tried to, all students learned about social movements by participating in one that they cared about and created. They wanted to be there to make these things happen. They got angry when they didn't happen and when others disagreed with them. It was real.

Teacher, presenter, and *New York Times* best-selling author Dave Burgess wrote the book *Teach Like a Pirate* in part to showcase how he tries to make every face-to-face meeting with his students something they would show up for even if they weren't required to. This memorable experience is what I want for my students.

I constantly ask myself, "What do I do to make the learning an experience? What do I do to make it authentic? What are my most innovative, successful learning adventures? What opportunities do I create to let students make their own memorable experiences?"

These memorable experiences don't have to involve using technology, but the technology available today could facilitate this process, and make them even more engaging.

My students have used Twitter to connect with real people in faraway places. For example, students have hosted a Twitter chat to show mastery of the class content. They talked with me to create seven questions and led a nation-wide discussion about civil rights topics. Another class of students used an online discussion tool to discuss and debate gun control issues. Students from Wisconsin and Ohio did research on different components of the debate and discussed them by typing their conversations, reading, and responding in real time. One student asked to call his congressman's hotline as I displayed it in class and explained our responsibilities as citizens to share our thoughts with our elected representatives. Of course, my answer was "yes," so he called and talked to someone in Washington D.C. right there from his desk in Room 250.

Students have used the freedom to do real things to ask questions of big companies when they need help. For example, when they were having trouble making their Animoto videos with their iPhones, they contacted the company and asked why some photos get cut off. The company's response didn't fix the problem, but it did explain the reasons for it. Students have also promoted causes they care about on social media and used infographics they have created using online tools to spread the word. They have created and shared anti-bullying videos that have been seen by thousands of people and probably influenced thousands more. They have connected with family friends to ask about career decisions, contacted national organizations to ask how they can get involved, and talked with professional game-creators to discuss the benefits of video games and possible career opportunities. They have shared videos of themselves singing to get auditions for nationally televised shows and reached out to college coaches to find out more about opportunities to go to school while playing at the next level. Students have worked hard to see that we don't send them out into the real world *after* school ends. They are actually living in the real world right now. And school can be part of that real world. Students have identified real-world problems and tried to discover solutions to them. What else can we do to help students make their learning personalized and important?

In my classes I ask the following questions.

Does our learning
1. Create an experience?
2. Make it authentic and related to students' "real lives" ?
3. Connect with the world and improve the world?
4. Make something?
5. Focus on something important now and in the future?
6. This space reserved for other important yet currently undiscovered ideas

These are my questions about our learning. These are my rules for this semester and next. I'll try to follow them. These are my new "Pitzen's Rules," and I hope my students will still be talking about the results in thirty-five years.

CHAPTER 16: HOOKS

With a Little Help from Our Friends
by Teresa Gross

"Boom, Boom, Boom!" The sounds burst from the door. Screams erupted from my students. The lights were off, the shades were drawn, and we were gathered together in one corner of the classroom. What were we doing? Experiencing the text, "The Monkey's Paw," of course.

It was the middle of fall, and my 8th grade Language and Literature Class was deep into literary essay writing. Our focus was short stories of the horror genre. We had read "The Lottery," "The Tell Tale Heart," "All Summer in a Day," and of course "The Monkey's Paw."

After our hearts returned to our chests, the students unlocked the door, explored the closet, and found nobody. We resumed reading. Then even I was not prepared for what happened next. The door flew open and students literally jumped off their chairs as we all shrieked again. My colleague from next door screeched "But nobody was at the door!"

Throughout our text study, my students were loving the horror stories and engaging in meaningful discussions. *Why was change so difficult for some and not others? Why did people appear to have power and lead while others seemed to submit to it and be followers? What can be the result of a guilty conscious? From a literary perspective, what are characteristics of horror stories? What themes are developed and what lessons can be learned?*

Despite their interest in these action-packed short story thrillers, I found a significant percentage of my class was having difficulty drawing conclusions, analyzing text, and truly comprehending the implications suffered by the users of "The Monkey's Paw." Particularly the final scene where Mrs. White opened the door to find whatever had been pounding on the door had vanished into thin air. They were having trouble wrapping their heads around the fact that nobody was at the door. *Where did "it" go? Why did "it" disappear? Why wouldn't Mr. White want his son back? Why wouldn't he look normal?*

In my years of teaching, I have found building text sets and using reader's theatre are incredible ways to bring texts to life while at the same time providing scaffolding and facilitating greater understanding. This works particularly well for those texts that require higher-level thinking skills, such as drawing conclusions and inferencing in genres such as horror, fantasy, and science fiction. These genres frequently are a mix of reality and fiction; therefore, part of the reader's job is to distinguish between the two and make sense of a collision of real and imaginary worlds.

As we were reading "The Monkey's Paw," *SCOPE* Magazine just happened to have it as their monthly "Reader's Theatre Play." As I read through it, I knew it would be a perfect supplement to our short story. It was also an ideal text to create an "experience."

Prior to reading it, I spoke with my colleague next door and we made a plan. On my part, I would read the play with my class and create the mood for the setting and theme. I turned off all the lights, I pulled all the shades, and I even had spooky music playing in the background. I pulled us all to the back corner of the room away from the closet door and distributed issues of the magazine. By creating the world described, I was able to heighten their sense of suspense, increase the feeling of anxiety felt by the characters, and bring the darkness of the setting to life.

My colleague's job was basically to bang on the door at just the right moment and really bring that feeling of the horror story to life. We attempted to time it perfectly. Of course he was not in the room to hear where we were in the play, so we were going to be as in sync as possible.

It could not have gone better! At the exact moment that we were reading about the knock on the door, he banged on the door so loudly that scared shrieks burst from my students. Two of them ran to the door, unlocked it, and looked in the closet for who might be there. Not finding anyone, they returned to their seats and we resumed reading. What I did not know was he was coming back for more.

Suddenly, the door flew open and he yelled into the classroom. Later he told me that he saw every student lift off their chairs in surprise and panic. It was definitely an experience many of them will not forget. In fact one student kept saying to me for a long time afterward, "Remember when we read The Monkey's Paw?"

(Of course, we have to know our students and create experiences that they will remember while also realizing the times in which we live. We must always keep in mind that we should be careful and sensitive to not create a situation that would traumatize or harm a student's social or emotional well-being.)

Although as teachers we encourage close reading and teach skills and strategies to access text, sometimes the most effective way to gain understanding is reading something in a different format and experiencing it to the best of our ability. For example, I can read about riding on a roller coaster, but unless I actually have the opportunity to do it myself, I miss much of the experience. In education, the more our students can experience the learning, the greater understanding and higher engagement they will feel with the task.

Literacy is such an amazing content area to bring stories and texts to life. As language and literature teachers, we have the ability to change our classrooms or environments, to create the mood, to put ourselves in the character's shoes, and to "live inside the story" for a short time. Through literature we can build empathetic and caring individuals who develop the ability to consider different perspectives by becoming the characters they read about.

Our students can learn such a variety of life lessons that will benefit them both in the present and the future. They are able to experience possible consequences of making certain decisions through the exprerience of protagonists and antagonists in texts. As educators, the most powerful teaching we can provide are the experiences we create for students. We have so many opportunities to create experiences in these areas. When those opportunities knock, I hope we'll all be at the door!

Teresa Gross *is a 17-year veteran educator with a passion for igniting a love of literacy in her school community. She holds certifications in speech therapy, elementary education, literacy, and a degree in education leadership. Teresa is a connected educator, co-founder of Coffee EDU Rochester, and creator and moderator for numerous online communities focused on teacher professional learning. Most recently she created #PD4UandMe, a weekly Twitter chat focusing on personalizing professional development for educators.*

CHAPTER 17: EDUCATIONAL TECHNOLOGY USE

She Was The Moose Of Her People
by Jason Bretzmann

I loved those speeches. I learned from those speeches. We all did. The high point was Brandon's lecture on D-Day that spanned parts of two class periods. He expertly drew the beaches and the obstacles on the chalkboard and explained each part of the invasion. Every student was on the edge of their seat. True story. And it was one of the few high points in my one-year-only career as a world history teacher. I drove forty-five minutes twice a day the following summer to take classes and get certified in sociology so I'd never have to teach world history again. Sociology and United States history would instead be my thing. But those speeches. How do I include those amazing speeches?

Let's try. Switch from World War II to the U.S. Civil War. Make a list of important topics. Give some student choice. Let the research, creativity, and speech-making begin. Popcorn ready. Smile on. Ready to be wowed.

The results? Disappointing, if I'm being generous. Awful, if I'm being honest. With a handful of exceptions, the whole thing fell flat. It was like watching the unremarkable remake of Dirty Dancing. All the right parts were there and it should have worked, except it made me want to put *everybody* in the corner.

Reflect. Reiterate. Try again.

Let's try "Stuff Boxes." Similar topics from the speeches, but this time every student gets a box and they stuff it full of stuff related to their topic. Stuff you could see, touch, hear, smell, and taste. Then they would talk about and explain their stuff to students as students walked to each box. These were not so much speeches, but descriptions, connections, and explanations of artifacts.

The results? Not bad, but a lot of work for students trying to find, make, and manage the artifacts. There was an intensive focus on meeting all the requirements of the stuff and on the managing of the stuff and it distracted a bit from learning the content. We were closer, but we weren't there yet.

Students did research and they presented their stuff well. It incorporated multiple intelligences and used all the senses. But it wasn't perfect. Their explanations weren't showing that they were getting a lot better at research. Their presentations weren't showing that they were understanding topics as deeply as we wanted.

And then someone mentioned that there was this new technology called PowerPoint. It was for making better presentations, and would solve all our problems and make our research projects perfect. This was going to be great! The thing we've been looking for to make this thing perfect. The technology would solve *all* our problems.

We went through the whole research process. We talked about how to present, and what the requirements were. We shared the rubric ahead of time and gave students a peer and self-evaluation. We were excited about the potential for what this could be.

In one of the first presentations, a very determined student proceeded to explain to us that Harriet Tubman ran the Underground Railroad and she was known as the "moose of her people."

I said, "The what?"

She replied, "The moose of her people," as she pointed indignantly to the screen where "Moose of Her People" was proudly displayed.

"Are you sure you don't mean the Moses of her people," I asked, "because, you know, she led them out of captivity."

"No, the Moose," she insisted. "That's what *it* said."

I knew immediately that this technology was not our silver bullet to fix education. As the presentations continued, I realized that while things were different, they weren't necessarily better. Modern technology is amazing, and it can do so many things. But it can't do what great teachers do. It can't make good decisions.

I reflected and reiterated again. I refocused our efforts on the things we want to see our students do and the content we want them to learn. I intentionally refocused us on both the journey and the destination. The learning process is important. And the outcome of that process and how we show the learning is important. The research, learning, creation, and presentation of learning continued to improve with each successive tweak.

But it's not about the technology. The technology is sort of near the end of the process. It's a tool that helps us show and share what we know. It can't solve all of our problems, but it can help us showcase what we've learned.

I've been using technology for decades in my classrooms, and when I talk with colleagues and help with what technology tools to use, I like to ask two important questions. What have you decided to teach? How have you decided to teach it? If you can answer those two questions, I can help you navigate through all the technology that exists so that you can achieve your goals. I don't have all the answers, but each teacher in the classroom does. The answers to what you want to teach and how you want to teach it can direct you toward the right technology to help, and the right technology to make the outcomes visible. It shouldn't happen the other way around.

Figuring out the what and the how can be an empowering for each of us as we grab control of the process. If we sprinkle in a little "Why?" into that process and include a useful technology tool that will help us create and share, we can feel those high points that we all want on a regular, continuous basis. Whether technology is part of the process or not, we'll keep iterating to get to those special moments where we can say that we loved that process and that outcome. "I learned from it. We all did."

CHAPTER 18: EDUCATIONAL TECHNOLOGY USE

Show Me The Munny
by Kenny Bosch

I remember certain lessons from my elementary education like they were yesterday. In third grade we churned and made our own butter. Why? I'm not exactly sure. Maybe it was a lesson on Wisconsin history. Does it really matter? I don't think so. Our teacher brought in all of the ingredients and a small churn. We discussed how to make butter, and then we tasted the butter we made on crackers or bread. The experience was what mattered. Participating in something unique is what made the experience a lasting one. When I think of the educational experience that students have in my classroom, I want at least one unique experience for the students every quarter.

We have almost unlimited options for our students today due to amazing educational technology. My school recently bought 3-D printers. I had seen students creating their own projects in the class that used them and thought, "How can my students use the 3-D printer in our history class?" Similar to the butter churning experience, I wanted my students to be able to create something and take it with them, instead of creating something for me, to leave with me.

What could we create with the 3-D printers that could relate to history?

"Show me the money!" I'm pretty sure it's illegal to print real money, so we were going to make "Munnies." Munnies are small, white, 3-D toy figures that you can buy at most major retail stores and customize to be any character you want. "What would be a fun way to use the Munnies in a history class," I thought? What I came up with was "Historical Figures Munny Project."

Each student received our version of a 3-D Munny to design in their own way. Next, they would research their historic character and put their research into some form of ed tech tool and present their Munny and the research they had completed to others in small groups. This project checked all the boxes: students had voice and choice, they were going to practice their research skills, they had to be creative in both the design of their Munny, and be creative in their use of ed tech to present their project. Most importantly, they were going to have fun. An experience. When we give students the power to make as many decisions as possible, the learning becomes meaningful. All that I had left to do was put the project in motion.

I contacted the engineering teacher at my school, Karen Lindholm-Rynkiewicz, and asked her if creating our own Munnies was a possibility. She told me she would find a model that worked and we began to make prototypes. We experimented with a few versions until we had it right and were ready to make enough for all of my students. Creating the Munnies was a long process taking 24 hours to make 12 of them. About two weeks later, the Munnies were ready. Now all I had to do was present the project to them in a unique way. Maybe a little mystery and a sense of danger would get them on the edge of their seats?

An odd-shaped, long triangular box with the words "Danger: Open Contents with Caution" written on it would do the trick. I created this box and had it prepared to be delivered to my classroom by my principal, Mr. Todd Irvine. He came into the classroom in a panic and said, "This box is very dangerous!" He set it in my classroom at the front table and then left. To heighten the drama and a sense of danger surrounding the box, I used some official yellow "Caution" tape and wondered out loud what might be inside the mystery box. Students were slightly scared and confused, but I assured them that everything was fine and that the box would be removed by the end of the day.

The next day, the box was still there. It stayed on the desk for over a week and each day the students would ask me about what was in it. For four days students asked me again and again if they could open the box. I continually looked for ways to push their anticipation to a fever pitch. Since this puzzling box was close to my microwave, when I reheated my coffee I used a yardstick to move it away from the appliance. I mused about my fear that the contents of the box might have a problem being so close to the radiation. I told the students that if an administrator did not take the box by Friday morning, we would open it. Finally, the time had come to look inside this scary box.

I asked, "Who is brave enough to open the box?" Hands flew up and the students gathered around the mysteriously dangerous box. I gave the brave souls gloves to wear to help make sure they were safe. Once the box was opened, they pulled out some random items including some crumpled up newspaper, the Munny head, a straw, some wire, and then the Munny body. Along with the random items was a small note telling them to go to my Twitter handle, @kennybosch, for a message. Once they were at my Twitter feed, they saw a message telling them to go to my YouTube channel for a video message about the items. Students were excited to watch the video and learn about the contents of the box and what we were going to make with them. I wanted to continue the feeling of suspense and mystery for as long as possible. Once students watched the video, they were excited to create and keep their own Munny.

Students could make their historical Munny based on anyone, real or fictional, past or present. In my classroom, we had created a culture of risk-taking and students had almost unlimited choice. Students could choose to create a Munny based on a politician, author, musician, athlete, actress, cartoon character, and so on. No limit to their choice. Students had instant buy-in and excitement because they were in control. Students asked me questions about their possible characters: "Can I make a Munny based on SpongeBob?" "Yes." I said. "You can make your Munny look like SpongeBob and research the creator of the cartoon series, how many years the show has been running, and how many movies, video games, and spin-offs were created related to this T.V. show."

More questions popped up as a student asked, "What can we use to color the Munnies?" I told them that they could use any medium they wanted to. Immediately students began to talk to each other about who they were thinking of creating for their Munny project. They began to research their historic character and look up key information. They saved numerous pictures of their character to a Google Doc to use as a reference when designing their Munny, and they collaborated on how to design both the Munny and their ed tech presentation project.

As the week went on, students became more and more creative with their projects and how they were going to demonstrate their learning. All year we had been using numerous ed tech tools, and those prior experiences were about to pay off. Students came to class excited and prepared to share their passion for their Historic Figure Munny project.

Students were ready to share all that they had researched and learned by preparing engaging ed tech presentations of their work. The variety of Munnies was amazing: Dr. Who, Mickey Mouse, President Teddy Roosevelt, numerous professional and Olympic athletes, Rosa Parks, Neil Armstrong, Batman, Thing 1 and 2, and more. Their creative uses of ed tech made every presentation unique. Some students wanted to have their Munny in the same scene as their real-life character. Using our classroom green screen and our iPad app TouchCast, we were able to make this a reality. We placed the Dr. Who Munny and his telephone booth on a green cart and used the green screen to place the Munny into the T.V. scene.

Another student researched Marie Antoinette, the last Queen of France before the French Revolution. The student had created her own guillotine and used a stop motion app with her iPad to recreate the infamous end of her reign. She then took the video and posted it to her own Wix website. The student that researched Rosa Parks created the Munny to look like her and brought in a Fisher-Price school bus. On the bus was a QR code that took you to a Lesson Paths series of linked videos about Rosa Parks and her influence on the Civil Rights movement.

Even more impressive than the creative use of ed tech was the passion students had for their projects. Students came alive when they presented their projects. A male student that rarely spoke in class discussions had created a Batman Munny. His Munny was impressive, but more than that, he had brought in a full-size Lego Bat Cave for his Munny to live in. Each person was supposed to speak to their group for five minutes and he could not stop talking about everything Batman. He knew *everything* about Batman: when the comic series was created, how the storyline regarding Batman had changed over the years, how many movies were made, who were the main actors, and on and on. He told me, "I could talk for hours about this stuff!"

The choices he had for this project created all of the drive he needed.

Did he learn anything? Of course! He learned how to read and sift through multiple websites for content and accurately cite them in his project. He worked on his soft skills of public speaking, eye contact, and how to read an audience. He created an ed tech project, a Google Sites website to curate his extensive research. But, did he develop any history-related skills? Yes! He developed his skill of historiography by analyzing changes in the story of Batman over time. He discussed the economics of the Batman series and how much comic books cost when the series was first created, comparing it to how much the most current movie grossed. As I looked around the room throughout the day, I was impressed by the effort, creativity, and passion the students had for the projects. In the end, they were the ones who were able to "Show me the Munny!"

CHAPTER 19: EDUCATIONAL TECHNOLOGY USE

Hello Kitty

by Josh Gauthier

Hello Kitty and I have a special connection. Yes, you know the iconic Japanese feline. Every time I see that silly little cat I can't help but smile, because it reminds me of one of the most impactful risks I ever took as a teacher and the students who took that risk with me. Where does Hello Kitty fit in with ed tech? Well, we should probably start from the beginning...

When I was a new teacher fresh out of college, I knew I was supposed to use technology, but we didn't spend a lot of time talking about the proper integration of it. That mindset, combined with the overwhelming nature of the first years of teaching, led to a lot of basic implementation that more or less was there because I thought it should be there, not because I thought strongly about the purpose. That all started to change during my second year of teaching.

Being a member of the district tech committee, as well as an expected leader in the building with tech (yeah, I know, crazy in just my second year!) meant I had subs several times a quarter for meetings or conferences. It always bothered me that no matter how well I set things up for the sub, the tasks I hoped would be completed often weren't. Whether it was a bad direction, a missed setting, or something else, it seemed there had to be a better way to have my class run when I wasn't there. After I attended the SLATE (ed tech) conference in Wisconsin, the answer was clear: I needed to make screencasts!

The session where I got the idea was about flipping the classroom, but using screencasts where I explain things to my kids when I was out of the room seemed like a powerful use of the technology. While I was not ready to take on a flipped classroom in that exact moment, there were plenty of places little screencasts could make a difference. It saved me from repeating directions and helped students who were absent get filled in without drawing my attention from other students. It truly was a revolutionary tool to use.

Another session that really stuck with me, and was the second of three key steps, was one titled "Breaking Down the Walls." The story was of a school near Milwaukee, WI that decided to literally bust down some walls to combine three classrooms of math students and run a self-paced math class in their middle school. Students worked through a computer program while having opportunities for small group instruction and then demonstrated content knowledge through checkpoints before being able to take assessments and move on. Wheels in my brain started spinning—what would this look like in *my* classroom?

To back up a few steps, I was a business education teacher. At the middle level, this meant that I would have most classes that lasted one quarter. After that, I would repeat the same content with another group of students. That meant many of the screencasts that I made could be utilized from one quarter to the next. Definitely worth the time investment. As the third quarter of that pivotal second year was getting underway, my views continued to change on how I could use these screencasts to an even greater potential. The third major step of this change happened at Edcamp Madison, Wisconsin.

At that Edcamp, I took a risk and attended a session about "Blowing Up the System." The teacher who proposed this wanted to buck back against the current system for schooling. *Who decided we had to teach these things in this way over this period of time? Can't it be reworked to run differently?* In discussions here, one thing was clear—I had power to make changes in my small little classroom that could let students take control while still having them learn the things that were expected.

Upon returning, I was on fire. How could I combine screencasts, breaking down the walls, and blowing up the system to make my classroom into the vision I had in my mind? Sitting down and thinking through all of my content, I was able to distill 50 unique skills I wanted my students to master in 7th Grade Computer Applications. While taking this inventory, I realized that I had created screencasts for many of these skills. It was settled. This project would be launched in the fourth quarter of this school year. Go big or go home!

Students would need to demonstrate their learning of these 50 skills through the use of screencasts or other artifacts. Opening the class involved a pep talk video (I think I even used the Kid President one) and spending time walking them through the setup of a Google Site where they would house their "evidence" of learning. One thing I strongly encouraged was not to simply use those skills for my class. If we were learning about how to use bulleted and number lists, I wanted them to use them for their English paper, not some invented context in my room. With that, we were off and running.

Students chose which skills to start on and where to go as they finished. Screencasts were popular, but many were of the silent film variety as we owned one working microphone! Aside from this, the class ran remarkably well. The high flier students pushed beyond the fifty skills I came up with and pursued many enrichment opportunities. Other students who struggled staying with the group did a terrific job enjoying their own pace. Even the students who caused behavior problems in other classrooms were not an issue with me as classroom disruption was almost impossible in a class where I was rarely leading the entire class through one thing.

It wasn't a perfect system. There was little excitement, no collaboration, and no big projects that required a synthesis of ideas. But the basis of something great was there. Now, you must be asking, "What does Hello Kitty have to do with all of this?"

The next year of that class, I had a student walk in and challenge me: "Name something that there isn't a "Hello Kitty" version of. Never really paying much mind to Hello Kitty, I simply said "Toothbrush." This student jumped onto Google, and in seconds, I was staring at a Hello Kitty toothbrush. Her joy over this topic was fascinating. In fact, she was into all sorts of quirky stuff, including preferring the nickname Megatron. Ultimately, Hello Kitty brought it all together for me. It was truly the essence of what this was all about.

I realized that the most important pieces of my set up were the ample opportunities for student choice and the ability for them to use their interests and passions as a way to demonstrate their learning. While a full-blown, self-paced class like the one I created isn't something I'd recommend for everyone, I would challenge everyone with this: if a student in your class loves Hello Kitty, how is your class set up to allow them to use that passion in their learning?

Josh Gauthier is ever passionate about how we can better educate children and is always looking for new ways to engage students. As a former business educator, he taught from 3rd to 12th grades. Josh is currently a technology training specialist for the School District of De Pere, WI and is excited about influencing teacher collaboration and having a greater impact on student achievement. Josh has participated in and organized several Edcamps, and has presented at conferences such as ISTE, SLATE, WEMTA, TIES and the Midwest Google Summit. Ultimately, Josh wants to see every student succeed. Connect with him on Twitter @mrgfactoftheday

CHAPTER 20: EDUCATIONAL TECHNOLOGY USE

Useful *In* School?
Or Useful *Beyond* School?

by Jason Bretzmann

"Why do you hate posters?"

I got that question as I was making suggestions for how students could show and share information about themselves for the opening get-to-know-you activities. My answer was long and winding and full of explanations, connections, and a focus on the long view of their educational careers and beyond.

I explained to my students that it's not that I hate posters, or even that I dislike them. It's more that I don't see the usefulness of them for most people. Perhaps for art students or those who like and are already good at drawing. Perhaps there are those who excel at cutting out or tracing letters from stencils. Perhaps there are glue-stick virtuosos who need to practice their craft of sticking things while making other things sticky. Perhaps there is someone who simply likes making posters.

I told my students to ask their parents, their grandparents, and the other adults they know, "When was the last time you made a poster?" My guess is that the last time they made a poster was in school. I don't have a problem with posters, but if we're going to practice a skill then maybe that skill should be something that transfers to something useful in our lives, in our careers, or in our future learning (college, career, and life readiness).

We shouldn't make things *in* school *for* school if we can do better. If we can do more. I asked my students, "What if we make things in school that transcend school?"

I continued. Imagine presenting your pitch before the board of directors as they sit around the conference table and you show them your poster with glue stick and cut-out letters. Imagine showing your learning in front of your college professor while holding and pointing to your poster board with extra glitter. Imagine applying for admission to the university, or for that scholarship that will keep you out of debt, but not finding a place to submit your 22" x 28" masterpiece.

I continued, "What if you created a digital representation of yourselves that used an online tool?" The product you would create could be aesthetically pleasing, simple to create, and professionally constructed. It could include information organized graphically, with pictures, video, and other information. As constant learners, you would have to understand or pay attention to design elements and could change or improve them easily as you work toward a perfect composition. You could share your creation beyond the walls of the classroom or building. You could paste a link into an online submission form (with no sticky mess). It would take the "What else should we know about you?" answer to a whole new level.

I pointed out that there are effective and ever-changing online alternatives that can help students create a professional-looking infographic about themselves or about any topic. If you have the opportunity to use these tools, I told them, you probably should.

What if you created this online resume using the technology effectively and you included the link on your traditional resume, or you had the shortened, customized URL at the ready so you could share it anytime and anywhere? Imagine that.

"Do you have a visual resume, Mr. Bretzmann?"

[Pause] "Yes. Yes I do. And I'll show it to you tomorrow."

At home that night, as I created my visual resume, I thought this could be helpful for students as they try to stand out in a sea of others? Presenting themselves visually with the latest technology tells a lot about who they are and who they could become.

So let's push our students a bit out of their comfort zones, and let's get out of ours. Let's give students opportunities to create visual representations that are useful now and in their futures. Let's encourage our students to practice skills that could set them apart as they create professional looking infographics. Let's not worry about hating the poster, but instead focus on loving the other options.

CHAPTER 21: EDUCATIONAL TECHNOLOGY USE

Oh The Places You Will Virtually Go

by Kenny Bosch

Growing up, I knew I wanted to go to college, but I didn't really have a plan. I loved basketball and the popular teams of the time became the universities that I wanted to attend. Even though I was a fan of these basketball teams, I didn't know anything about these universities, the campus life, the degrees they offered, and so on. I didn't have family members to give me advice in this area, and the internet was not the powerful research tool that it is today. What would have helped me to make a more informed decision would have been an opportunity to visit these universities and get a hands-on feel for the campus. So, why didn't I visit some of these schools? Time and money were the hurdles my family and I were unable to cross.

Time was the first major obstacle. I grew up on a farm in Wisconsin as one of seven children. I was the first male in my family to go to college. My father worked a 5AM-5PM job and then came home and worked on the farm. We were all expected to work on the farm and help out in any way that was needed. The universities I was interested in were as close as six hours away and as far as 40 hours away by car, and I knew we would never fly to any of these schools. As the realization came to me that we were never going to have the opportunity to have my father take off time from work and the farm to visit schools, I narrowed my collegiate search to a much smaller area.

Even if we had the time, I knew my family could not afford to travel to Michigan or California simply to visit colleges. Visiting college campuses is an investment by families in their children's futures. My father and mother fully supported my desire to go to college and were proud of me for wanting to be the first male in our family to do so. The larger issue with going on a campus tour was the expense involved in traveling to these schools: lodging, the cost of meals, and other expenses. When I thought about the distance my family would be willing to drive in a day for a college visit, I again narrowed my search area to a distance about three hours from my home. Ultimately, I was able to set up one college visit and that is the college that I attended.

As I thought about my personal experience I decided I wanted to use ed tech to help my students have better opportunities for researching and touring college campuses.

The first time I saw a VR (virtual reality) headset, I knew it could be used in life-changing ways. Our school had a professional development day set up and one of the options was to research an idea you were interested in. I spoke with my administrator about finding ways to incorporate VR headsets into our learning. At the time, I thought about using VR headsets for social studies research and virtual field trips. What came out of my PD day research was the VR College Tour project.

My own lack of options in visiting college campuses inspired me to look into VR college campus tours for my students. I found that there are a lot of websites and options for prospective students to use when researching colleges and universities, but nothing was as powerful as a VR experience. I began to find a few apps that gave students the best experience while using a VR headset. I spoke with my administrator about my vision, and he agreed to let me buy some headsets. Two weeks later, my students were ready to go on virtual college visits.

VR college tours have changed my students' perspective on their possibilities of going to college. Watching students put on a VR headset for the first time and "walk" the campus of a school in another state is a fun experience for everyone. Students were a little apprehensive at first and some even said, "I already know where I want to go to college. Why do I have to do this?" I encouraged them to give it a try and research two colleges out of state, two colleges in state that they have not visited, and to research one college that they have never heard of before.

Soon after putting on the VR headsets, students were immersed in a different world. Some students were up and walking on the campus of faraway schools or standing in old and impressive libraries.

Others were looking from side to side inside a dorm room in a school they have never heard of. They could use the VR headsets and virtually sit inside a classroom at some of the best and least-known universities in the world and get a real sense for what it would be like without ever spending any money or time traveling to these schools. One of my favorite moments in this project was when a student who told me she was "100% sure" of where she was going to college took off her headset and said, "Oh no! I really like these other schools now. Now I'm not sure that is the only school I want to go to!" The VR college tour was more powerful than I had even imagined.

The day after we finished the VR college tour project, I had the class fill out a Google Sheet and discuss what they learned about each college. Students were explaining the pros and cons of each university from their perspective, the degrees they were interested in (or their lack of degrees for their future), and whether or not they wanted to actually visit the school. One male student I spoke with said that because of this project, "I now think I want to go to college. I hadn't really looked into it." Another student said, "I always thought I wanted to go to school in Wisconsin, but now I want go out of state." A student that believed she was going to be offered an athletic scholarship to swim at a university far away from Wisconsin used the VR headset to visit the campus. Afterwards she decided she did not like the aquatic facilities at that school and did not want to spend the time and money to officially visit.

At the end of the hour a student approached me and asked if he could take the VR headset home and research some more colleges and show his parents. He thought, "If I show them that I am serious, maybe they will let me attend the college I want. Maybe if they use the headset to see the school, they will want to actually take me their on a real visit?"

After using the VR headsets and college tour with my junior classes, I decided that exposing students to these college tours as freshmen would be even better. The second year of using the VR headsets for college tours involved all of my students. Every student had an opportunity to research and virtually visit colleges of their choice. My administrator saw the power of these virtual campus tours and had me meet with Student Services to see how we could expand their use throughout the school. The use of VR headsets as an ed tech tool has provided numerous opportunities for our students to explore options they may have not otherwise considered. With the help of ed tech, the very real concerns of time and money needed to visit college campuses has virtually been eliminated.

CHAPTER 22: EDUCATIONAL TECHNOLOGY USE

Triple Moving Kahoot!
by Jason Bretzmann

Whether it is with a group of adults, high school students, or elementary kids, we seem to all react to a Kahoot! or other competitive digital review game in a similar way. A question is displayed, we compete feverishly to answer quickly and accurately, then when the correct answer is revealed, there is an immediate hubbub and generalized guffaw that rises up from the crowd. A quick smile-filled discussion ensues with the nodding and good-natured taunting of people-in-the-know following close behind.

In my best experiences with this online quiz-game tool, I have used that moment of peak engagement to deliver more content and put the questions and answers into context. I've told my students that it is perfectly normal to react after the reveal, but then we have to simmer down quickly so I can deliver more information and move onto the next question. It's a dance we do of balancing the serious fun and the serious information dissemination. And it works.

Students seem to love the experience. As they enter the room, I have the ten-hour YouTube video of Kahoot! music playing to get them in the mood. It only takes a few notes as they walk in to get a, "Yes, Kahoot! today!" from the first few entering students. Of course, there are other similar tools and they will all continue to be updated, added to, and improved.

And yet I couldn't get past the idea that it was not a perfect experience for everyone. What I noticed most is that students who are not "winning" the game are not as engaged as those who are. (An educator-friend also mentioned to me recently that her son tried to *lose* a Kahoot! after a couple of his middle school chums loudly mentioned that he won the last two. I guess you don't want to be the guy in middle school who always wins the Kahoots!).

So, I thought, if winning or trying to is part of the engaging part of the Kahoot! experience, how do I keep those at the losing end of the game at their peak engagement as well? Furthermore, how do I keep those who start late or have problems with their internet connection intensely involved when they know they probably can't be the winner.

I decided to refocus the students' idea of winning. It is partly about using a growth mindset. It is partly about shortening "the game." And it is partly about what seems to be a pretty good philosophy for cross country runners: catch the person in front to you. (I've never run a competitive race or coached others to do it, but it sounds right, doesn't it?) With those ideas, I created The Moving Kahoot!

I hyped it up. Told students they wouldn't want to miss it. Explained that it had never been done before, so they would want to be part of history. Plus, they would get to review for their state-mandated civics graduation test. They asked, in a mildly excited way, if it was another Kahoot! I told them it was a Moving Kahoot! and then let them try to fill in the missing explanation on their own.

When they arrived for the Moving Kahoot!, the music was playing, but the room looked different. For one of the few times all semester, the desks and tables were in rows. I numbered the desks from 1 to 30 with printed numbers that I cut apart and taped to each desk top. I told students to choose any spot to start the game. After the bell rang, I turned down the music, displayed the game that I had set up on another tab, and welcomed the students to the Moving Kahoot!

I explained that in just a few moments we would be starting the Kahoot!, and that students should join with their first name and last initial because we want to know who you are, but we don't want creepy people on the internet to know who you are.

I continued to explain that this is just like a regular Kahoot! because there is one winner. At the end of the game, only one person can be the winner sitting in the chair labeled with the number 1. But that's not all, I explained. There are differences. The biggest difference was that after every five questions, everyone will move to the spot in the classroom that corresponds to their position in the game. The top five players will be in this row. The top ten can be found here. As I walked toward the higher numbers, I explained that this was not a way to point out who was ahead and who was behind. It was a way to give everyone a chance to keep playing because the focus was not to get to number one (although that's a fine goal), but the focus was to catch the person in front of you. Only one out of the thirty of us can sit in that first seat, but each of us can try to catch the person in front of us. If you're at seat 11, try to get to 10. If you're at seat 21 try to get to seat 20. If you're at seat 30, first blame it on the slow Wi-Fi, and then try to get to seat 29. I explained how in education we call this a growth mindset and that it's something that they can apply in their other classes and throughout the rest of their lives: *I'm not there yet, I'm going to keep going, I'm going to bite off little pieces and always make progress.* And then after another five questions, we'll move again.

Students were skeptical at first, but moved after the first five questions. Then after five more they moved again. After every five questions students began to move like they had done it this way all their lives. It re-energized the Kahoot! experience and allowed all students to be successful as they tried to catch the person in front of them. Even those that were victims of a slow internet connection and were relegated to the highest number rejoined and tried to get themselves to the low twenties in the room. It was a successful innovation on a great game, but it wasn't the last iteration.

The Triple Moving Kahoot! was the next step on our journey toward continued engagement. We used the two 26" inch televisions I got for cheap on Black Friday along with the Smartboard screen to create three distinct locations for our Kahoots! We set up Court 1, Court 2, and the Stadium Court at the Smartboard. Students again entered the classroom to the Kahoot! music, but this time they went to one of the three locations. Students faced the Smartboard in the front of the room, or one of the smaller televisions in the corners on the opposite wall. This way, they were facing away from each other so they could play three separate games. I told students that they should be honored to be part of the first Triple Moving Kahoot! in North America. I said it's never been done before and who knows, it might be a huge failure. They might hate the whole thing. But let's try it anyway and see what happens.

With the same principles described above, we played as many eleven minute games as our class time would allow. After each game, the top three players in the game moved one court toward the Stadium Court for the next game (except for those at Stadium Court who didn't move), and the bottom three players in the game moved one court toward Court 1 (except for those at Court 1 who didn't move). By the third game, we had pretty competitive groups at each court who were differentiated at similar ability levels.

In the Triple Moving Kahoot! students were able to employ a growth mindset because they could see that even if they didn't win one game, they could still compete and work hard in the next one. We shortened the game so students would have a chance to get to the top of the next one in case they had a bad connection or a rough start to their game. We gave students the opportunity to catch the player in front of them and compete with similarly effective and motivated students. Students were engaged because everyone had repeated chances to be successful.

I still can't get past the idea that it's not perfect yet, but maybe that's just me having a growth mindset. Maybe I'm just trying to catch the player in front of me. Maybe with the next iteration I will.

CHAPTER 23: THAT ONE KID...

On Our Honeymoon, Elliott Joins Us for Dinner
by Jason Bretzmann

"Hey, Mr. Bretzmann. It's Elliott. Are you still up for getting something to eat?"

We had just arrived at the hotel after a ten-hour flight to Hawaii. Married for two days, this was the first night of our honeymoon.

"Yes," I said. "We'll meet you downstairs at the burger place."

I had met Elliott years before when he was a sophomore in my U.S. history class. He was a good student and a good kid who was not always appreciated by his classmates. He was mature in many ways and made strong connections with his teachers. It took his peers a few more years to appreciate him to the same extent.

As his teacher in high school, you felt like you had to be there for this kid because he had the potential to be great. But he also had the potential, without guidance and the right relationships, to go off the rails. Maybe that wasn't really the case, but it felt like that at the time.

He made the juvenile mistakes of a young person trying to find his way. But overall, he was a neat kid who *was* finding his way.

I stayed connected with him throughout his high school years. He took my sociology class. He was my student aide during his study hall. I watched and listened as he connected with his chorus teacher and his AP Government teacher, a marine.

During study hall Elliott told me the history and values of his new passion, the United States Marine Corps. He explained the trivia, the stories, and facts he found interesting and important. He told me how he was going to be a marine. During that semester of study hall, I didn't get a lot of work done, but I heard all the details of the adventures Elliott was planning. I saw pictures of the awards he won for having the most knowledge of his most revered branch of the United States military. (I'm pretty sure he won them all.)

After his graduation, Elliott proudly became a marine and was deployed for two tours in Afghanistan. It must have been an amazing and frightening adventure. He did it admirably and effectively. A good kid who followed his passion and became an impressive man.

Elliott and I stayed connected. He periodically invited his other teachers and me to the local professional baseball games to talk, reminisce, and watch some baseball together. We all went.

After his career in the Marines, it seemed unlikely that Elliott could return to the pedestrian lifestyle of his home town. Instead, he headed to Las Vegas and became a craps dealer at a local hotel and casino. He enrolled in law school and passed the bar. He called periodically and we would talk politics. I had a background in politics and had become the school's government teacher, so we had a lot to talk about. Eventually Elliott told me he was going to run for the state assembly, and I asked where I should send my contribution check to his campaign.

Elliott served again. As a multiple-term assemblyman in the Nevada state legislature, he initiated and shepherded many important bills to become law in his state. He was a well-respected member of the legislative body and decided to retire after being elected to legislature in four regular and four special sessions. He'll be able to focus even more on his clients and their legal needs now.

"Hey, Mr. Bretzmann. It's Elliott. Are you still up for getting something to eat?"

Some teachers say that they wouldn't want to live in the district where they teach because the kids are always there. I usually say that our students are actually everywhere. Then I tell them the story of how I went all the way to Hawaii and met up with my former student. On our honeymoon. I tell them how he was stationed there as a marine, and that he bought a disposable camera to document the event. He asked my newlywed wife to take pictures of him and me.

"Hey, Mr. Bretzmann. It's Elliott. Are you still up for getting something to eat?"

"Yes." Always. Everywhere. Every time. And when we get together again, I'll remind you how proud I am of you. And I'll secretly think of the other kids like you who have found their way, followed their passions, pursued their dreams and found success in the service of others. I'll explain how I'm impressed by the things you've done and how I'm in awe of the people you've helped along the way. I'll tell you how honored I was to go to dinner with a former student, how happy I've been to watch you grow into such a positive role model in your community, and how wonderful it has been to add a small part of that process.

CHAPTER 24: THAT ONE KID...

Michael Becomes My Little Brother
by Brianne Neil

Every teacher has that one kid. The one who makes your entire career worthwhile. The one who gives your career purpose. You were meant to be an educator for the sole purpose of teaching that one kid. Mine was Michael. A tall, goofy, kid walked into my third period eighth grade science class on the first day of my first year of teaching, and the story of my one kid began.

He wasn't the top student of my class, but did reasonably well. A report card full of A's and B's, while putting in lots of effort to stay out of the C's in math, was typical for him. He was a prominent student athlete on campus, playing both basketball and baseball, so grades were important to him in order to remain eligible. Grades were also very important to his parents. I had been in communication with his parents from early on in the year. On his first progress report, I left a comment of 'excessive talking' which prompted an immediate phone call from his dad. It wasn't long into the conversation when I realized that Mr. Thompson was a stern man with a no-nonsense attitude. Originally, the comment was left simply as a heads-up to his parents that it could become a problem in the future. I quickly learned to be more intentional and transparent with parent communication.

While it's true that Michael was rather talkative, he always made us laugh. Looking back, I think he was covering up his own insecurities, whether they be academically or socially, with humor, often poking fun at himself. He really began to enjoy my class and we had started to build a very positive teacher-student relationship. Over the course of the fall semester, he began bringing his lunch to my room. He even kept packages of mayonnaise for his sandwich in my desk drawer in case he forgot it downstairs. I left extra snacks or candy in the bottom drawer for him to take and eat before practice. I had class at the time of his lunch but he would just sit at my desk and eat, listening to the lesson all over again, often answering questions along the way or throwing in some detail I left out. The veteran teacher in me now rolls my eyes at that first year teacher.

Basketball season began right after Thanksgiving. All the starting lineup players were my students, and he was definitely one of the star players. He asked me to come to every game. Although it wasn't always convenient, seeing the boys light up when they saw me in the stands made those long days worth it. I met Michael's parents in person for the first time at the first game. Michael got his self-discipline from his father, but his playful demeanor from his mother. After inviting me to sit with her, Mrs. Thompson said it was so nice to finally meet me as she heard about my class every day. She admitted that she didn't even know my name for the longest time because Michael always referred to me simply as "Ms.", a detail that still hasn't changed.

Michael's biggest struggle in school was math. In early spring, he began to worry that he wouldn't pass his state assessment in April. So he asked if he could start coming in before school for me to check his homework and let him work on extra test practice questions. My dream since I was a little girl playing school with dolls and stuffed animals was always to teach math, so I jumped at the opportunity! His parents were very appreciative of my extra time, but I was more than happy to help him out.

I would get to work around 6 a.m., my eyes still heavy, to get a few things ready for the day, and he would come in at 6:30, full of energy. Sometimes he brought us breakfast. He learned that I am not really a morning person, and it takes a little bit of time for my coffee to kick in before I'm ready to have full conversations. So we would sit side-by-side in silence, both working, until he had a question. Then, he would cautiously reach across the desk for my cup, slosh it around a little to gauge how much was in it, and then determine if I had had enough caffeine to process his question. If it was still over half full, he would set it back down slowly and say, "Nope, not yet."

Needless to say, he made it through 8th grade, passed his state tests with flying colors, and was ready for high school. I wasn't sure I was going to see much of him again but was excited for the opportunities that awaited him. When I was a student, I never really called upon my former teachers. I was self-sufficient, had a good support system of family and friends, and never looked back. I guess I thought it would be the same for my students. I took care of him for nine months, I was no longer his official teacher of record, and I assumed my job was done.

But this was only the beginning of our story. Over the summer, I received an email from his mom. Michael's summer baseball league games had started, she shared his schedule, and said I was always welcome to come watch and keep her company on the warm summer nights. I took her up on the invitation and, while walking up the bleachers towards her smiling face, I slowly started to realize this kid would be more than a former student.

In high school, Michael played basketball and baseball all four years. And although I couldn't make it to every single game, I certainly tried to. His mom had become a dear friend of mine over the years, sharing our lives sitting on the bleachers cheering on her son. Mr. Thompson was more reserved, and much more focused on the games, but we had a mutual understanding and respect for one another. He appreciated the support I provided and the influence I had on his son. She was Michael's biggest cheerleader, and he was Michael's harshest critic.

I continued to help Michael with his math, and often times other subjects as well. It wasn't uncommon for me to swing by his house after practice or, once he could drive, he would come over to my house with his backpack and a list of questions. He always hoped I had a nice meal or treat ready and waiting for him, but after I burned a batch of sugar cookies once, I think his expectations of my cooking skills became more realistic. The 'excessive talking' had certainly not changed. No topic was left undiscussed. He would share everything with me during our study sessions, from relationship struggles to arguments with his dad, funny things that happened at school and major updates on other students I had taught. He shared with me his dreams of playing major league baseball and the fears associated with not making it. He even promised me a brand new car when he made it big. Our relationship had become more of a sibling bond as he grew up. He was the little brother I never had, and I took on the role of the protective older sister.

The fall of his senior year he was offered a scholarship to play baseball at Sam Houston State. I was at my brother's house, about to sit down to dinner with my family, when my phone rang. I remember stepping outside, into the cold air, and Michael said, "Well, they want me." I was so excited for him. He was going to college. For a kid that was really only in school for athletics, this was big news. His family had visited the campus, toured the facilities, and said it felt like the head coach was offering the world on a silver platter. He would have access to tutors to keep him focused on school and the best trainers to continue to prepare him for the next phase. He had a phenomenal senior baseball season, going deep into playoffs, and as graduation approached, one chapter was ending while a new exciting one was beginning. Again, I wasn't sure how this new phase of life would affect our relationship, but I was so proud sitting with his family as his name was called at graduation. Walking across the stage, he found us in the crowd and raised his arms in celebration. I would be lying if I said I didn't have tears in my eyes.

The following day, Michael was drafted to the Pittsburgh Pirates minor league team in Florida. Now he had a decision to make—college or the league. As soon as he called with the news I knew deep down what his final decision would be; I knew he wouldn't say no to the first step of his dream come true, but he promised he would think about it. A few weeks later he was on his way to Florida. I was apprehensive. Part of me wanted him to go to school and take the opportunity to create a future for himself after baseball, but it seemed that all the pieces were falling into place for him. The kid I met five years prior was now a young man on his way to living out his dream, and I couldn't have been more proud of him.

We talked off and on the first few months he was away. He was a little homesick at first, missing his family, his friends, and his high school sweetheart. But with a busy schedule of workouts, practice, and traveling for games, exhaustion was the overall feeling. I received a knock on my door late that fall. I don't even go to the door if I'm not expecting anyone. Then, my phone rang and it was Michael, asking me what I was doing. When I replied that I was at home, he said, "Well then, answer the door!" It was him! He had just driven in and said that I needed to be his first stop. He completed his first season and was back home for the winter. I swear he grew three inches and aged ten years while away. He walked right into my house like an old friend, pulled out a snack from the fridge, and sat down on the couch, making himself at home.

A couple weeks later I met him and his mom for dinner. They said they had news for me and wanted to talk. It wasn't unusual to meet them for dinner, but the circumstances seemed odd, and I didn't have a good feeling about it. As soon as I arrived at the restaurant, he and I made eye contact, and from the deep sadness in his eyes, I knew something was wrong. Apparently, while Michael was in Florida, his mom was diagnosed with breast cancer. She already went through a round of chemotherapy and radiation and was in remission. They hadn't told him because they wanted him to focus on baseball. They hadn't told me because they didn't want me to have to lie to him.

She was doing well when it was time for him to leave for his second season in Florida. He hated being away and would come home as often as he could, but she insisted he go play baseball. Don't worry about her, she told him, this is your time. We would occasionally talk on the phone or text while he was away. He would send me pictures and tell me stories about his teammates. During the off season, he would come back to Houston, work at his dad's company, and keep up with his workouts. There was talk of moving him up to the next level and he was hopeful it would happen when he returned. However, when it was time for season three, he was uneasy about leaving his mom. The cancer had come back and had spread. I never really knew the extent of it at the time, as he never liked to talk about it, and she wasn't well enough to tell me herself. She was still insisting he pursue his dreams of baseball, so he left, but his heart just wasn't in it the same way. Her treatments were proving unsuccessful and Michael decided to come home. He left Florida, left the team, and returned home to spend time with his mom.

I got a phone call one late October night. As soon as I saw it was from him, I knew. All he said when I answered was, "She's gone." He had just received the news and was on his way to the house to see her. The next day he showed up at my house with ice cream looking for a place to hide from it all. The sadness had returned to his eyes, and I asked him "What's next?" He said that he thought it was time to go to school. His mom was gone, but he was heading out on a new journey. Some moments stick with you forever. You remember every detail. Hugging Michael after his mother was lowered into the ground at the cemetery was one of those moments.

Over the next few weeks, his agent made phone calls to various schools, seeing what options were available to him and talking to coaches and trainers across the country. In January he was enrolled as a student at Louisiana State Alexandria. Michael would be ineligible for that season due to his experience in the minors, but if he kept his grades up and met all the team requirements, he could play the following year. Going back to school was an adjustment after a couple years off, and the tutoring sessions resumed, this time over the Facetime app. Of course, the dream of playing in the league was as strong as ever.

Michael is still in school working towards a business major. He comes home for the summer, but I'm already helping him with apartment hunting for the fall. Who else is going to walk him through the steps of applying for an apartment and explaining the importance of good credit? He still calls for help editing papers, checking equations, and even advice on girls. He still just shows up on the doorstep. And yes, he still calls me, "Ms."

A boy, with a head full of dreams, walked into a brand new teacher's eighth grade classroom. For nine months she was his classroom teacher, but for the last nine years, she has been more than that. 'That one kid' made all the difference, for both of us, for all of us. His journey continues and I plan to be in the stands ready to support him in whatever he does next.

Brianne Neil, *a graduate of Texas A&M, is currently entering into her tenth year in education. While teaching science and math for eight years, she discovered that life lessons were really the most impactful to her students. Brianne's passion for helping kids realize their full potential and discover their unique abilities has spilled over into her newest role, a high school curriculum coach, as she mentors teachers in their own journey to grow as educators.*

CHAPTER 25: THAT ONE KID...

Tom Learns Sign Language
by Tracy Kelly

When I was a 1st through 3rd grade teacher specializing in students with autism for a large district, I would often visit with the kids and teacher in the neighboring autism Pre-K/Kindergarten class. We shared stories, heartache, and strategies. This other teacher had a student, Tom, who I often saw urinate outside of the classroom in a corner. He was in kindergarten at the time. I offered suggestions but often got, "He does it in the corner *inside* of my classroom as well. I have tried everything." I kept making an effort to help but didn't find much success in trying to positively change the situation.

The following school year, Tom was placed in my classroom. I thought that since he was now in 1st grade, he might be a little older and perhaps a little wiser. It turns out, he not only urinated in the corners, he periodically "watered" the plants as well. Not only that, but Tom did not speak. He preferred to yell and scream, or he would just grab someone's hand to take them where he was trying to direct their attention. Got it! He had communication issues that no one had addressed. I wish I were as quick of a learner as this story makes it seem, but it took me a week or two to figure it all out. Probably most of you were already thinking of ways to help me solve this problem.

I was still an intern teacher in my second year of teaching. My first year, I only had five kids and all of them were verbal. My undergraduate degree was in economics, and boy, was I overwhelmed. I needed a strategy that would help with Tom's lack of verbal abilities. My wife, a special education teacher, helped me determine that American Sign Language (ASL) could be something useful to try. What a great resource she was (and still is).

I spent a weekend figuring out how to teach ASL. I started the process that following Monday with *Baby Signing Times*, by Rachel

Coleman. I did this with our whole class. We learned ASL during the same time slot that we normally had a speech language therapist come into the room, but on off days.

We were trying additional strategies as well. Three things were going on at the same time: we started using ASL to teach Tom and others how to ask for common things at school and home, we started using a bathroom break every 30 minutes for Tom, and we introduced a bathroom icon that students could get and bring to an adult in the room. As Tom was non-verbal, we already had his daily schedule in an icon format anyway, so we just taught the bathroom as an additional icon.

As we were hearing less screaming and having fewer wet corners in my classroom, I sent a note home to Tom's parents asking if they wanted me to send some videos and other resources. They answered yes! I sent home videos, printed ASL signs, and other information. I thought that if they used them, great. If they didn't, then no biggie. I tried.

We continued using *Baby Signing Times* in a more advanced way, as the kids and I were learning to be more proficient. I often times found myself outside of class, talking and using my hands at the same time. Not just with the kids, but staff and parents alike. (And yes, I still do this often, even though I no longer teach that type of class.)

When parent-teacher conference day finally happened, Tom's dad showed up. It was the first time I had ever met him. He hugged me and thanked me over and over. He started to cry and shared with me that they had never learned to communicate with their son until I sent home the videos and ASL signs. They no longer had screaming and yelling at home. They could now communicate their son's needs and wants together. While they still had a lot to learn, Tom's dad said they were doing much better as a family. Wow! I still tear up writing this.

As a teacher, I knew that I was truly where I belonged. I was able to help a family communicate. I changed their trajectory in life. I changed mine, as well.

As happens so often with our families with disabilities, they move away. A few weeks after the conferences, Tom's dad invited me to their house. I had never been to a student's house, but I wanted to go. I needed to go. This was when Tom's dad shared that they would be moving away. As a child, I attended a lot of different schools, too. I understood. I was sad, and Tom's dad expressed that they were as well. He thanked me again for changing their lives. We parted ways, and I never saw or heard from them again.

Even though they moved away, I think of Tom often. I'm proud and thankful that I was able to play a part in helping to impact a family's daily life in such a positive way. I like to think that Tom is out there having a positive impact on others as well. I'd love to see Tom and his family again and share that while they probably felt that I did so much for their family, it was their family that I will never forget, as they changed *my* life forever.

Tracy Kelly *has proofed and edited four books as he learns how to write for himself. He has earned a bachelor's in economics, a master's in special education, and an Ed.D. in candidacy status while he writes his dissertation. Not bad for a high school dropout. He lives with his wife, and their two sons. He also has an adult son and three cute grandchildren.*

CHAPTER 26: THAT ONE KID...

Jamie Bites Teachers
by Dr. Patricia Kolodnicki

Excitement and nervous anticipation filled the summer days as I decorated my first classroom. Obtaining that job was my first challenge, but what I was to find out was that I was going to face a more difficult one.

When class lists were distributed, each teacher met with the principal to review their list, carefully describing the history of each student, receiving insights on family history, siblings, strengths, and struggles. When the principal got to Jamie's name, she paused. Her lengthy story continued for fifteen minutes and included highlights of her biting her first grade teacher, behavior issues, and an overall record of poor grades throughout elementary school thus far. She had also recently been placed in a resource room to help her with her reading and math.

I listened intently, silently thinking through how I would try to meet each challenge and help Jamie move forward on her educational path. I was appreciative to have all this information, but as a daughter of an elementary school teacher, I just kept recalling my mother's important words, "Everyone starts with a clean slate." That would be *my* challenge, and I hoped I could step up to meet it.

The year was a blur, looking back on it now. The first few days with my fifth graders were filled with getting-to-know-you activities like taking their pictures for a bulletin board, or working on developing class routines and rules. Jamie was there, of course. Her appearance was in direct contrast with her reputation. The sweet-faced 11-year-old had her hair braided, braces newly placed on her bright white teeth, and her studious face was framed with a pair of blue, wire-rimmed glasses.

While her classmates kept their distance, obviously aware of her past reputation, I made it a point to get to know her. She proudly told me about her first grade teacher and how she knew that all other teachers were scared of her. I tried not to show my cards, so I put on airs that it was certainly not my first class ever. Certainly not! I was certainly confident in my abilities to teach. Certainly. On one of the first few days of that school year, I even said that I had learned a lot about how they have done things as students in previous years. But I also told them that none of that mattered to me. What mattered was what they chose to do now, this year.

I continued to learn more about Jamie and her family. Her younger brother was a star student. Jamie had dreams of becoming a dancer. Her mother and I spoke regularly on the phone. I would let her know about her daughter's latest grades, including her improving progress in math, my favorite subject. I reported on her behavior as well. I knew that I needed to get ahead of any issues we may have in the future, so constant communication was essential. The school seemingly assisted in my endeavor of getting to know Jamie more by placing her in my before-school tutoring group to prepare for the upcoming math and English exams.

I believe a turning point in our relationship came in early December when I arrived to school one morning, and a disheartened smile displayed my own set of shiny silver braces. While there is nothing like having braces for the second time at the ripe old age of 22, the students seemed to be able to relate with me on a different level. Especially Jamie. The calls home became less frequent throughout the year, but they always ended in the same way. I would tell her mom that things were good and that she would be okay. The rest of the year was a whirlwind of writing and reading, math projects, and science experiments. The school year ended as they still do, with hugs and smiles, and wishes of a fun summer and a successful next year.

The following year, Jamie's sixth grade teacher came to me knowing her reputation, and asked me what led to Jamie's improvements. Her behavior, attitude, and academics took an impressive turn. She definitely wasn't the old Jamie. I said I brushed off any knowledge of the previous Jamie. Clean slate. I just kept commenting on how hard she had worked to get where she was now.

Years later, I caught up with Jamie on social media. Jamie was nearing high school graduation and explained to me how well she did in her classes and how she was planning on attending a performing arts college. I wished her luck, knowing full-well she wouldn't need it.

A few years after that, when I noticed Jamie was promoting a performance on social media, I secretly bought a ticket. I watched that young woman performing on stage, singing and acting with her friends with a smile on my face. During intermission I posted that I was at the performance, and when it was over, I had a message in my inbox to find her in the lobby. She was a bit taller than I remember, with a beautiful smile, and the same fierce tenacity in her eyes. Her parents hugged me warmly. They were so proud of who she had become. They made a point to mention that it was fifth grade that turned her around. I argued that it was not fifth grade or me that made the change. It was Jamie who decided that she didn't want to be the person she was before. All Jamie needed was someone to give her a clean slate so she could really be who she wanted to be.

It wasn't Jamie's first year, but it was mine. I thought I'd have the challenge of Jamie to deal with that year. Instead it was Jamie who had the challenge of doing better. She rose to the challenge and exceeded it. I'm glad I helped in that process by taking my mom's sage advice and giving Jamie the opportunity to write her own story about who she was going to be without the hindrances of past stories of who she had been. That slate has been filling up positively for years now, and she continues to add more and more to it.

***Dr Patricia Kolodnicki** is a learner, researcher, and special education mathematics teacher from Long Island, New York. Over her 15 year career, she has maintained that giving up on a student is not an option. Currently Dr. Kolodnicki teaches at Salk Middle School, recognized as a National School of Character, an award she was instrumental in achieving. Graduating from LIU with an Ed.D. in educational leadership, her passion towards and involvement in the educational community continues.*

CHAPTER 27: THAT ONE KID...

Steve Builds His Confidence
by John Briese

You can read all of the books and study all of the strategies that can help you prepare to become a teacher, but nothing will prepare you for the first time a student is brought to tears in your classroom. This happened to me before I even had my own classroom, while I was substituting during my last year of college. I was doing all I could to prepare for my future career, and I learned early on how challenging, yet rewarding life as an educator could be. Only weeks into my first experiences in a classroom, I faced one of the most pivotal moments of my career.

My entire career as a full-time educator has been in secondary schools, but on this particular day I was substituting for a second grade class. The assignment the teacher had left involved the students presenting to their classmates the information they had been learning. In a whole-group setting, students presented one at a time. All was going well until we got to Steve.

I had noticed Steve was almost completely silent the entire day, but I still called on him when it was his turn. He nervously asked, "Do I have to?" I responded with what I thought was an encouraging, "Yes, you'll do great". As soon as Steve turned around and saw all of the other students looking at him, he broke down crying. I froze. My inner-dialogue spent a few frantic seconds thinking, *My classes haven't covered this yet*! Then I stopped trying to overthink it, and just tried to quickly do what I thought would be best for this student.

I pulled Steve aside and asked another student to begin presenting, trying to distract the rest of the class so he could regain his composure. However, when Steve and I got to the back of the room, he felt the rest of the class looking back at him, and he began to cry harder. My heart has never raced so quickly as it did in that moment.

My own fear of not being able to control the situation sunk in. We both calmed down, though, as we walked out to the hall where we could have a more private conversation. As I started into my, "It's going to be OK" spiel, I tried to brainstorm a way to remedy the situation.

I quickly devised a plan that I hoped would allow Steve to gradually build his confidence. I asked him who his closest friend in class was. He told me and I quietly pulled that student in the hall while the other presentation was going on. The three of us talked for a short time, then I asked Steve if he felt okay presenting his information to his friend. He did. I stood in the doorway facilitating the presentations in the classroom while Steve discussed his information in the hall. After a successful presentation to his friend, I asked Steve who else in the class he was very comfortable with and brought that student to the hall. After Steve's second presentation, I brought all the students back into the room and broke the class up into groups of five to six. Steve and his two friends got a few more classmates in their group, and Steve presented his information to them successfully. My thrown-together plan to gradually help him build his confidence had worked, and fortunately it didn't end there.

Having modified the whole-group presentation to a small-group setting, the presentations that were supposed to last 40 minutes ended in just under 15. Twenty-five minutes of unstructured, unplanned time to a novice substitute teacher is the definition of fear. At this point I was the one almost in tears...

I chose to have the students mix up their groups so that they could present their information to new students. This sounded like a genius plan until I thought of forcing Steve into a difficult situation again having to present to a group he was not comfortable with. This didn't even cross my mind when I broke the groups up. It is amazing how the fear of unstructured time can cloud your memory so quickly. As I scanned the room to find Steve, I saw that he had chosen to be the first person in his new group to present their information. I watched intently, and as he finished, he and his groupmates struck up a conversation about something else and were laughing and having fun. I cherish this memory and can still see Steve laughing with his classmates only minutes after being so scared to interact with them that it brought him to tears. I have thought of this image many times since then, mostly at the end of a bad day to help me regroup and recall the rewards that this job can provide.

This day was one of the most rewarding days of my career as an educator because it was the first time my decisions helped a student overcome an obstacle they were facing. However, it is also the day that I learned that when you hit a wall and do not know what to do, always focus on whatever is best for your students. I couldn't have cared less whether Steve presented his information to his classmates that day, or if he was able to soak up what his classmates were teaching him in their presentations. While his tears were rolling down his face, all I wanted was to find a way where he would be comfortable in the classroom. My goal had 100% to do with his emotional needs rather than his educational needs in those moments, and *that* was the ultimate lesson that I learned that day.

Throughout my career I have had to pull students aside and have discussions with them that had nothing to do with their education and finding success in their learning. They had everything to do with trying to find a way to help them find happiness. Steve taught me that, and I am forever grateful. What I learned from him has helped me build more relationships with my students, and has ultimately made me a better teacher.

We are hired to teach our students specific content that they need in order to be successful in their lives, but sometimes it is the content that *isn't* in the curriculum or the textbook that is the most important. Sometimes it is teaching our students lessons like how to gain confidence amongst your peers or how to develop a social relationship with those around you that will change their lives forever. Unfortunately as a substitute, I was not afforded the ability to watch Steve grow. The next year I got a full-time job at a high school and did not return to Steve's school. However, I know how much he taught me, and helped me grow not only as an educator, but as a person. That is the reason that Steve might be the most important student I've ever taught.

John Briese *began his career as an educator in 2010 teaching English and graphic design, and has spent the last few years as a technology coach helping teachers integrate technology into their classrooms. He spends his spare time with his two young children and getting in 18 holes of golf whenever possible. Joining Twitter as an educator changed his life, and he will encourage you to join every chance he gets.*

CHAPTER 28: THAT ONE KID...

Clarence Learns *And* Teaches
by Leigh Anne Geib

He was that kid. You know. The kid who didn't quite fit in. The kid who seemed a bit lost among the crowd. He was that kid. You know the one. The one who was always unprepared. He was that kid. You know. The hungry kid. He was *my* kid. He was the misunderstood kid. He was the untrusting kid. He was the tough one. He was the kid that had the biggest wall around his heart, and I was determined to knock it down. And I did. I thank God every day that I did. And I thank my student, Clarence, for trusting me and for letting me in.

Clarence came to me as a ninth grader. He was one of those kids who I just felt something with. I knew that despite his many guards and attempts at not being noticed, that he was going to be somebody. We first bonded in Language Arts class. He wanted to be invisible and would sink in his seat to listen to his music and attempt his work. He didn't sink low enough, however, to avoid my questions about his song choice. His face lit up when he learned that I, too, love the band *LIVE*. He was shocked to hear that my favorite song was also "Lightning Crashes." If you've ever heard this song, you might be puzzled. The song can be interpreted in different ways, but in reality the song is about the circle of life. The song is about rebirth. At least, that is how Clarence and I chose to think of it.

You see, Clarence had a hard past. He had a lot of skeletons in his closet. The cross he carried was heavy. He needed that song and the tune of his life to be about rebirth. The more we got to know one another through class and literature, the more I had the pleasure of seeing him blossom. I'll never forget when we read *The Outsiders* together. Clarence isn't exactly a big fan of reading, but this book captivated him. As a class, we would talk about conformity and identity. He expressed that he was truly a Greaser. The book truly moved him, and I sometimes have to laugh when I think back to how mad he was when he found out Johnny dies.

As the days and eventually years went by, we were able to work together through his academic and personal struggles. For the longest time, Clarence was always made to feel as if he were "less than." He was always made to feel that there were mountains he just would not be able to climb. What Clarence needed was a cheerleader. He needed someone to say "Why not" instead of "No." Most importantly, he needed an adult who he could trust and someone who trusted him in return. What he needed was someone who would judge him on the content of his character and not what was written in his IEP or on a disciplinary record.

Through the years, Clarence and I had many breakfast meetings. It was how he chose to start his day. One day in class, he accidentally called me "Mom." We laughed so hard at this slip. It was one of those moments where I wished I could have said something more but didn't. A few days later he just started calling me "Mom" and asked if I minded. I really did not mind but for once, I had no words! I form strong relationships with my students. I don't know how it happens, and I don't question it. Some people have negative commentary about this, and that is fine. However, I truly believe that being an educator is a blessing and an honor and regardless of your religious beliefs, even Clarence needs a "mom."

As a freshman, his senior year had seemed decades away. Before we knew it, it was here. Clarence had gone from being an immature young boy to developing into a fine young man. He even made the honor roll! When he first made the honor roll, his eyes filled up with tears. He had never seen anything good about himself on paper before. He had experienced a regeneration and a rebirth, just like in his favorite song.

Clarence taught me a lot about the power of compassion and the miracle of grace. He just needed someone to believe in him. He needed someone to be there for him and accept him for who he was in that moment. It's no surprise that I cried like a baby at his graduation. We had our last school selfie in cap and gown and I'll never forget it. To me, the picture reflects a journey. Talk about growth!

Even though he is no longer at the high school with me, we are still in touch. He told me at graduation that I changed his life for the better. I beg to differ. He changed me. This young man who felt so undeserving of anything good, let alone love, ended up teaching me in return. Clarence taught me that there is no such thing as a hopeless situation. Clarence taught me not to just listen to a student, but how to hear them. Clarence taught me that even though lighting may crash…an angel does and will open her eyes.

Leigh Anne Szczurek Geib was born and raised in Philadelphia. Leigh Anne completed her undergraduate work at Mansfield University. She is presently teaching High School Special Education ELA for Palmyra Area School District and has been doing so since 2005. Leigh Anne recently graduated summa cum laude M.Ed. through Eastern Mennonite University. Leigh Anne resides in Central Pennsylvania with her husband, Mark. They have two children, Elliot and Nora.

CHAPTER 29: THAT ONE KID...

Sidney and His Phone
by Aubrey Jones

After the first months of school, I was needed to fill a new role in the district, so I was transferred to a high school placement in November. As I looked at the sea of faces, I realized very quickly that I was between a rock and a hard place. The substitute teacher who had been there before me was popular with the students and told the kids that "no matter what, they would not fail." Apparently, I had a different message. Here I was with rules, curriculum and interventions.

Sitting in the front row was a student named Sidney. He rarely looked up from his phone, and I was sure that he would fail the class. Every day I was met with resistance, and I struggled to capture his attention. I tried talking to him after class, talking to his case manager, and changing assignments to accommodate his interests. I would stand near his desk while teaching. I tried to involve him in small group instruction. I gave extra credit assignments, and he never turned them in. I used sarcasm as an attempt to engage those who were more interested in technology and stated that I should bring in my pet unicorn next class (to see if I would get a response). Still, there was nothing. I was discouraged and frustrated, especially when he asked me for help and told me to hold on as he was finishing a game on his phone. I was sure that I had failed as a teacher.

Then when we came back after break, Sidney was the first one in class and he asked what we were doing that day. I told him we were doing a nutrition unit. His eyes lit up and he was instantly engaged. He contributed to class discussions, gave ideas for topics, and produced original, creative work. He was excited about learning. He found his voice in class and began to police the other students about being on their phones. Sure enough, he went and woke kids up as well and reminded them of appropriate phone usage.

He started to joke with me in class and even gave his opinions on the topics that we were studying and the things we were working on. My favorite example was when he gave quite a compelling argument as to why we should watch the movie of a book instead of listening to the audio book. In fact, he did research and saw that the person that did the voice over in the audio book was the same as one of the actors in the movie. He added that information to his appeal, and I had to say that he did present a very convincing argument.

From this one kid, I learned to never give up on building relationships and that every day is a great day to work on building trust. This one kid taught me that every day is a new day and the events of the day before don't count in the events of today. He reminded me that there is hope and even when I feel like no one is paying attention, there is one kid that *is*.

Sidney had no hopes after graduation and was content with his life the way it was. His life revolved around the events of social media, and he did not care what was going on in the classroom around him. There was nothing else that was important except for what was happening on the screen in front of him. Class seemed like an inconvenience.

One day Sidney looked up from his phone and I saw the curiosity in his eyes. He looked like he had a question. I waited. I was okay with waiting for his question. The silence sucked; it seemed eerie and I wanted to break the silence so badly. However, I decided to sit there and wait. Instead of entering his world and prying, I waited for him to enter mine. He eventually got tired of the silence and came into my world with a question. Granted, it was five minutes later, and my answer was something that I had already said. But there was an opening.

It didn't take long for Sidney to start asking me repeat instructions on a consistent basis. He asked over and over again until he understood exactly what was expected from him. That was progress. I would start at the beginning and go through. Sometimes I felt like a VCR as I was asked to stop, rewind, or fast forward. Even though it was sometimes tedious, it was progress. Sidney actually wanted to know what to do and how to do it. At that point, Sidney would ask his questions, get his answers, and then he would go back to his screen. However, sometimes, he took an extra few minutes to talk to me about something we were learning or even the score from the latest game. Caring about and asking about things was progress. And the progress continued gradually and built upon itself. He was headed in the right direction.

Sidney started to have hope for and make plans for life after high school. He got himself a part-time job at a fast food restaurant to offset the costs of attending the local community college. He found a sense of responsibility and a sense of belonging. Most importantly, he has learned to advocate for himself, his needs, and his education.

I have learned so much from Sidney. I learned numerous lessons as a teacher and the importance of being a human being first. I watched him struggle but instead of bailing him out, I waited. This was huge in both my teaching practice and in the way he learned to approach the class. With my support, he had to do this for himself. And before that, he had to decide that he wanted to.

I took away a lot from Sidney. His phone became less important than my class or what I had to say. It had been a defense mechanism so that he could keep his cool persona and not look like a fool in front of members of his class. He did not want to appear dumb or stupid and wanted to avoid the attention. He would have rather been the class clown than be known for asking questions or be seen as someone who cared about school.

However, as we neared graduation and he realized that most of these kids would not be at the high school in the following year, he took the time to invest in himself and his education. There was no longer fear when he asked me to repeat myself. There was a genuine desire to do things right. He realized that he needed to unplug his phone and engage his mind in the world around him. He was exactly where we wanted him to be now, and he had made the decisions to go there.

As I began to look back on our year together and all the trials and hardship that we encountered, I paused in my reflection and smiled as I thought about that one kid. That one kid that I reached during the year. The one kid that made the most significant changes in his education journey. The one kid that I will remember for my entire teaching career. He is that one kid that I will look back on and remember all the lessons that he taught me when I was supposed to be teaching him. He was that one kid that made teaching worth it for me that year. And this year, too.

Aubrey Jones *is a special education teacher. She doesn't believe in labels or excuses, but empowerment, growth, and opportunity. Each story is a chance to learn. Aubrey lives in Contra Costa County, CA.*

More from
The Bretzmann Group

PERSONALIZED PD: GAME OF STORIES

The game that is taking over every professional development experience to make it more fun, energizing, and collaborative.

Build capacity while building community with this unique and entertaining game. Hear the stories of your colleagues while reflecting on your own development as an educator. Get the conversation started about how to move your building and your district forward. Honor the professionals you work with every day by listening to their progress and their process as educators.

Everybody has something to contribute. Everybody has something to learn. You might win the game, but you might win more by losing!

Play *Personalized PD: Game of Stories* today and take your professional development to a whole new level.

Find this game at **tinyurl.com/gostories** #GoStories

FLIPPING 2.0: PRACTICAL STRATEGIES FOR FLIPPING YOUR CLASS

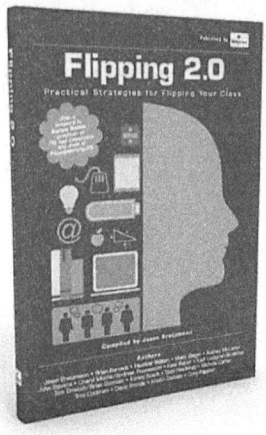

With a foreword by Aaron Sams. If you've decided to flip your class, you probably have new questions: How do I do this? What will it look like? What will students do in class? How will I create learning experiences for students outside of class? What have other teachers done?

Flipping 2.0: Practical Strategies for Flipping Your Class seeks to answer your questions. And it opens the dialogue for us to continue to learn together.

In this book, you will follow practicing classroom teachers as they walk you through their flipped classroom journey; why and how they made the change, what obstacles they overcame, the technology they used, and where they are heading next. As a flipped learning teacher, you need time to check out workable solutions that other teachers have created.

Look inside their classrooms and learn from their experiences. Watch flipped teachers at work. Pick the brains of those who've been there, and join the conversation. You'll find something useful in every chapter.

And there is a chapter just for you in this book, including English, math, science, social studies, world languages, technology, Google tools, mastery learning, elementary, middle school, part-time flipping, and even professional development. Read *Flipping 2.0* today and make your decision to flip a reality.

Find this book at **bit.ly/flipping20** and **tinyurl.com/flipping20**

*Please contact **jbretzmann@bretzmanngroup.com** for more information or for special discounts on any Bretzmann Group item when purchased in quantity.*

PERSONALIZED PD: FLIPPING YOUR PROFESSIONAL DEVELOPMENT

What should professional development look like? Can all teachers get exactly what they need? How do we energize every individual to realize their full potential?

Personalized PD: Flipping Your Professional Development helps answer these questions and more. Seven authors start from the premise that teachers are learners who learn at different paces and start in different places. Personalized PD helps each individual teacher move toward self-determined goals.

The authors take you through their experiences while giving you their best "pro tips" and most useful technology tools. They'll save you time and research by pointing you in the right direction right now. Each chapter gives you a window into how these practicing educators execute their plan to get every teacher what they need and move each individual toward their own plan of learning. Plus, short vignettes expand on and go deeper into the most useful tools and techniques.

Come join the conversation, and be part of the fundamental change in professional development we call CHOICE (Constant progress, Honoring professionals, Ongoing learning, Individualized focus, Collaborative learning, Energizing experiences).

Personalized PD: Flipping Your Professional Development will help you get there.

Find this book at **bit.ly/personalizedPD** #personalizedPD

PROFESSIONALLY DRIVEN: EMPOWER EVERY EDUCATOR TO REDEFINE PD

Traditionally in education, the letters PD have stood for an antiquated, one-size-fits-all form of professional development inflicted upon educators. Mandated to flock to the same location at the same time, they sit and get the same thing...whether they need it or not. Just mention the words professional development, and you'll get groans, eye rolls, and deflated educators in response.

Now, educators worldwide are on a mission to foster a movement toward personalized professional development and opportunities for true adult learning. With useful educational technology and a philosophy focused on a growth mindset, intrinsic motivation, and sustainable autonomy, the momentum is growing.

In "PROFESSIONALLY DRIVEN: EMPOWER EVERY EDUCATOR TO REDEFINE PD" Jarod Bormann shows us exactly how to effectively implement personalized PD using his successful model. It's the most extensive explanation anywhere. As a leader in the movement, Jarod lets us in on the process to redefine the letters educators traditionally dread into a true description of the best version of our educator selves—PROFESSIONALLY DRIVEN.

It is time to rethink adult learning and implement a model that helps create energized educators and leads to empowered student learners. Get your copy today and discover how to help yourself and your colleagues redefine PD while leading all educators to be PROFESSIONALLY DRIVEN.

Find this book at bit.ly/ProDriven   #ProDriven

bretzmanngroup.com
storiesinedu.com

www.ingramcontent.com/pod-product-compliance
Lightning Source LLC
Chambersburg PA
CBHW070810100426
42742CB00012B/2319